4888
.E641
P721
1991
c.2

COVERING the ENVIRONMENTAL BEAT
An Overview for Radio and TV Journalists

LOU PRATO

Poynter Institute for Media Studies
Library

APR 07 '94

ENVIRONMENTAL REPORTING FORUM

Washington, D.C.

Covering the Environmental Beat
An Overview for Radio and TV Journalists

Copyright © 1991 The Media Institute

All rights reserved. No part of this publication may be reproduced or transmitted in any form without permission in writing from the publishers.

First printing September 1991.

Second printing December 1991.

Published by The Media Institute, Washington, D.C., and the Radio and Television News Directors Foundation, Washington, D.C.

ISBN: 0-937790-47-8

Library of Congress Catalog Card Number: 91-66458

Table of Contents

Preface	vii
Introduction	1
I. Politics of the Environment	7
II. Television and Radio News and the Environment	31
III. Risk Assessment and Science of the Environment	53
IV. Where Do We Go From Here?	69
Notes	77
Acknowledgments and Selected Bibliography	81
Index	99

Preface

This monograph is the first publication issued under the auspices of the Environmental Reporting Forum (ERF), a joint program of the Radio and Television News Directors Foundation and The Media Institute.

In creating the Forum, RTNDF and the Institute recognized that news stories about the environment are growing in importance and are destined to be a major item on the journalistic agenda for years to come. However, with the increasing variety and prominence of environmental stories comes the problem of telling them thoroughly, responsibly, and comprehensibly. The best of tomorrow's health, science, and environmental reporters will become, in effect, more than mere reporters, guiding their audiences through a labyrinth of confusing and often conflicting data.

Covering a vast subject like the environment will require a reporter to grapple with extremely complicated technical material. The reporter will need to develop an understanding of the scientific process that may easily go beyond anything learned in school. The reporter will be forced to sift through facts, opinions, claims, and counterclaims from government agencies, business entities, and a host of sophisticated special interests.

Our goal is to make the Environmental Reporting Forum a positive force in this process. The Forum will explore current environmental issues and the problems of reporting those issues on radio and television. It will bring its findings and recommendations before the widest possible audience of professionals and the public.

Properly used, the tools of radio and television journalism can bring a story like the environment to life in a way unrivaled by any other medium. Through its publications, symposia, and other programs the Environmental Reporting Forum will be a valuable resource in helping broadcast journalists use these tools to their fullest.

David Bartlett
President
Radio and Television News
Directors Foundation

Patrick D. Maines
President
The Media Institute

Washington, D.C.
September 1991

Introduction

The environment has become the hot topic of the 1990s. One cannot watch television, listen to radio, or read a newspaper or magazine without encountering something about the environment and what we're doing to it.

Global warming. Clean air. The spotted owl. Disposable diapers. Fast-food packaging. The subject is all around us. And everyone from politicians to movie stars to housewives, it seems, wants to do something about it.

The specific issues are sometimes a matter of life or death—if not for us, then for generations yet to come. Environmental concerns are intertwined with almost everything we do: What we eat. What we drive. Where we live. Who we vote for. How much tax we pay.

The subject is vast and complex and fraught with contrasting values, conflicting agendas, and deep emotional beliefs. It often pits one branch of government against another. Corporations against environmental groups. Scientist against scientist. And now, more than ever, journalist against journalist.

Precisely because coverage of the environment is so consequential and so complicated, the responsibility and integrity of journalists involved in such coverage is vital. What they report influences public opinion and government leaders. That, in turn, can change laws and regulations. Shifts in public policy can force some companies out of business and make fortunes for others. They can destroy some people's jobs and sweep others into elected office.

Never has the need for fairness and objectivity in journalism been as crucial nor the trust of the public as meaningful. But journalists attempting to pursue balanced and objective reporting are often confused (and sometimes blatantly deceived) by the seemingly overwhelming "evidence" presented to them by the parties involved. Reporters lose their perspective and they ignore a fundamental rule of journalism: to be skeptical. Still other journalists zealously believe it is impossible to be objective about the environment; they feel a journalist is required to be an advocate, to draw conclusions no matter how valid the arguments may be from the other side.

This debate takes on even more significance in the electronic media and particularly in television, the medium for the masses. The ability of television to persuade and manipulate, intentionally or unintentionally, is thoroughly documented. Poll after poll continues to show that most Americans get their news from television and that they find TV news very credible.

Local TV news, be it over the air or on cable, has become more influential and more reliable as network audiences diminish. That amplifies the responsibility of local reporters, producers, and news directors—and, perhaps most importantly, local ownerships—when it comes to environmental issues. Here, however, many have fallen short. Many have done nothing. Many have been cavalier. And many have been simply negligent or incompetent.

Thus, one of the prime reasons for this book is to encourage more coverage of the environment by local TV stations. One can hope that local radio stations will be similarly inspired. Radio and television stations large and small must understand that there is a growing need for better environmental reporting.

There are a number of stations that already exemplify what environmental reporting can be. Although their styles and approaches may differ, they share one key trait: commitment. The personal commitment of owners, news directors, and reporters.

Resources—time, manpower, and money—must be allocated. People must be trained properly and given enough time to analyze an issue. Superficial coverage is easy and already too prevalent in television news. Coverage must be more than a reaction to crises. An oil spill or nuclear accident might focus immediate attention on a specific environmental problem, but it might also distort or exaggerate that very problem. TV's coverage of such crises usually does little to enhance understanding of the overall context or economic tradeoffs surrounding environmental issues.

This book is intended to be a primer and an initial guide for electronic journalists covering the environment. It is designed especially for those reporters and news directors who have limited experience in the environmental arena. It is meant only as a beginning, to help a neophyte become familiar quickly with the intricacies of environmental reporting and to understand the countervailing philosophies that politicize the coverage.

This is not a book about the issues. An abundance of material is available about specific environmental subjects. But this book does analyze how certain issues have shaped the media's coverage and the public agenda.

Chapter One—"Politics of the Environment"—explores the political ramifications of environmental journalism; the use and manipulation of the electronic media to advance and deter political agendas; and the perils of advocacy reporting.

Chapter Two—"Television and Radio News and the Environment"—deals with television's unique journalistic problems and power; the effect of TV news on public perceptions of the environment in the last 20 years; and a look at the current status of environmental reporting in local radio and television news.

Chapter Three—"Risk Assessment and Science of the Environment"—examines the theory and significance of risk assessment and risk management (the measuring of environmental risk against economic considerations); and the use and misuse of scientific information and sources.

Chapter Four—"Where Do We Go From Here?"—poses some questions about coverage of the environment by radio and television reporters in the 1990s.

References cited at the end of this publication should be used to further the reader's understanding. Two books published by The Media Institute, *Reporting on Risk* by Victor Cohn, and *Health Risks and the Press* edited by Mike Moore, should be seen as companion volumes to this one. So, too, should the Summer 1990 issue of the *Gannett Center Journal* on "Covering the environment" published by the Gannett Center for Media Studies.

The November/December 1990 issue of *Columbia Journalism Review* and the January/February 1991 issue of *Quill* have major articles on environmental coverage. One of the authors, Warren Brookes, is a syndicated columnist who has written widely about the environment and the controversies of news coverage. His articles and those of other prominent print reporters covering the environment—such as Jim Detjen of the *Philadelphia Inquirer*, Rae Tyson of *USA Today*, and former *New York Times* reporter Phil Shabecoff—can be obtained through Nexis, the Mead data retrieval service.

Detjen and Tyson are officers of the Society of Environmental Journalists, which publishes a quarterly journal that is loaded with summaries and tidbits about environmental journalism.

Another major resource is the Environmental Health Center of the National Safety Council located in Washington. It is directed by Morris A. (Bud) Ward, one of the real patriarchs of environmental reporting. Ward's guide to reporting on chemicals, *Chemicals, the Press, and the Public*, is a must for anyone covering the environment; his three-year-old monthly newsletter, *Environment Writer*, is an informative and objective monitor of environmental journalism.

A personal note. When offered the opportunity to produce this monograph I eagerly accepted. I remembered my first encounter with major environmental issues while an assistant news director and then news director for a Detroit television station in the early 1970s. PCBs were contaminating cows and their milk in the Michigan farmlands; industrial wastes and chemical run-offs were polluting Lake Erie and poisoning the fish. I recall very little about how my station handled the stories. I know that neither we nor our competitors did much in-depth reporting except for an occasional series. Certainly we were a bit naive. But the environmental movement was then in its infancy; the resources one can utilize today simply were not there.

Frankly, not much had changed in local TV news coverage of environmental stories when the Three Mile Island nuclear accident occurred in 1979. That story touched close to home since I frequently drove through Harrisburg and once lived within a few miles of the accident site.

Ten years later, I was in Washington running Northwestern University's graduate-student news bureau, Medill News Service, when the Alar apple scare erupted. As we covered that story for our client radio and TV stations, we thought we were well versed in the sophisticated public relations techniques of special-interest crusaders—but we were wrong.

I only wish someone had written this monograph 20 years ago.

I. Politics of the Environment

Politics, in the purest dictionary definition of the word, engulfs, saturates, and distorts virtually all environmental discussions. Only the naive or the foolish would believe differently.

Webster's New Collegiate Dictionary provides the words that characterize the politics of the environment: "Politics...the art or science concerned with guiding or influencing governmental policy...competition between competing interest groups or individuals for power and leadership in a government or other group...

"Politic...characterized by shrewdness in managing, contriving, or dealing...sagagious in promoting a policy...shrewdly tactful..."

Take any environmental issue from the sublime to the mundane and the politics is all encompassing. Everything about the environment appears to have a political tone. That's because there is no unanimity on how myriad environmental problems should be resolved or in what priority. As a result, thousands of environmental constituencies, special-interest groups, businesses, government agencies, and politicians—with ever-shifting objectives and personal agendas—

are constantly battling for the hearts, minds, and votes that determine public policy. Meanwhile the life of the planet is at stake.

The environmental field is so politicized that it sometimes seems everyone is suspicious of everyone else's motives almost to the point of paranoia. This tenet is basic to understanding why there is so much controversy, acrimony, and animosity about environmental issues and the media coverage of those issues.

Thus, reporters, producers, and news directors who get involved in environmental coverage must be forewarned. They, too, will be suspect. And if they *do* allow their own specific political perspective or biased point of view to impede their search for truth and fairness, their credibility with the majority of the public will almost certainly diminish if not disappear. They may well be revered by those with the same beliefs but others will mistrust and denigrate them.

Politicization of environmental issues is so prevalent that even scientists, policymakers, and public-interest groups that are normally credible and responsible are distrusted. Unfortunately, this lack of trust makes covering environmental issues very difficult for the reporter aiming for fairness. This is as true for an experienced environmental journalist with specialized training as it is for most general-assignment TV reporters and their news directors whose environmental knowledge may be limited at best.

The issues are often so complicated, contradictory, and technical that one can easily become overwhelmed. The best some reporters can do is to learn all they can and to be skeptical about everything. Not cynical. Just skeptical. Skeptical of government sources. Skeptical of science. Skeptical of corporations. Skeptical of environmentalists. And skeptical even of their own opinions, which should be subject to change as they learn more about each environmental issue.

Perhaps ABC's Roger Caras says it best. Caras has covered environmental issues for 35 years, specializing in animals and wildlife. He has been ABC's special correspondent for animals and the environment since 1974.

"Be careful not to get too emotionally involved and be careful of your own beliefs and opinions," he says. "I've made a lot of mistakes in 35 years because there were times I was so sure I was right and so certain other people were wrong. Accuracy is most important and should always be your goal. That can be extremely difficult if you allow your emotions and passion to interfere with your responsibility as a journalist."

Public Policy and Politics

Politics—as embodied by our elected leaders—always has been at the core of the environmental movement. But never more so than now.

It was Gaylord Nelson, then a senator from Wisconsin, who helped to create the original Earth Day of 1970 and turn it into an enduring environmental crusade. Earth Day 1970 spawned the Environmental Protection Agency (EPA) and the nation's first Clean Air Act. Twenty years later Earth Day 1990 helped to coalesce the opposing factions in Congress and the White House to finally amend the complex bill, a legislative impasse that had lasted 13 years.

By this time, the EPA had become one of the largest regulatory agencies in the federal government and was near to achieving cabinet status; a new Republican president had been elected saying he wanted to be known as "the environmental president"; several Democratic congressmen were using their pro-environment stance and their vocal environmental constituencies to boost their own presidential aspirations; and American taxpayers—most of whom do not know what the Clean Air Act actually does nor comprehend its economic implications—were committed to paying billions of dollars over the next decade to resolve controversial environmental problems.

The Clean Air Act exemplifies the politicization of the environmental movement. To many—especially those political compromisers of all genres—the Clean Air Act is salutary legislation that will help rescue the planet. But to others—particularly some environmental activists—it is a sell-out that doesn't go far enough. To still other special-interest groups—including many in the business community— the Act is an example of economic overkill that symbolizes personal self-interest and politics at its worst. Though proponents and critics may disagree about the merits of the Act, they concur that it is incredibly complex.

Morris A. (Bud) Ward, who directs the Environmental Health Center (EHC) for the National Safety Council, says: "In the past 20 years, it is the single most complex, most litigious of all the environmental laws. Arguably it has led to the most improvement of all these laws and unquestionably has led to the most compliance costs in the private sector."

To assist journalists through the legislative maze, Ward's office is publishing a "Reporter's Guide to the Clean Air Act." The guide follows an earlier well-received EHC handbook for reporting on chemicals, solid waste, and radon called *Chemicals, the Press, and the Public*.

Ward may well be the single most important friend of environmental journalists. He was an environmental print reporter for 14 years, and is friendly with environmentalists and reporters of all political philosophies. His EHC monthly newsletter, *Environment Writer*, is an excellent resource for journalists. In December 1989 he helped organize the Society of Environmental Journalists, whose membership is currently climbing past the 500 mark. In that context, his succinct opinion of the politics of the Clean Air Act is noteworthy.

"I love to hate the Clean Air Act," he says. "It is an extraordinary law. But it should not be put into a narrow cost-benefit perspective. What is the cost of each benefit? In that regard, the costs of it are easier to quantify than the benefits and that is why it is so controversial.

"Now, many environmentalist groups believe the benefits are worth it no matter what the cost. If you disagree with them, you're against them. There's no middle ground. We all want clean air. You should be able to criticize the means—the Clean Air Act—without criticizing the goal—clean air. But some environmentalists won't let you."

And the environmentalists form a powerful coalition at election time. They need the politicians to achieve their goals. They also need the media. The politicians also need the media to further their political agendas and to get re-elected. Thus, the media are used by both environmentalists and politicians as the means to an end. Of course, business and industry also use the media and politicians to influence environmental policy. In the midst of all this, one might rightfully worry that the public interest runs the risk of being neglected or abused.

The development of a policy to rectify an environmental problem does not mean one side is necessarily right and the other definitely wrong. Usually there is a struggle among a number of legitimate but conflicting philosophies, and often the resulting policy compromise satisfies few of the combatants.

Currently, there is probably no better illustration of this quandry than the controversy over the spotted owl. It pits idealistic environmentalists who want to save the owl as an endangered species against the beleaguered Pacific Northwest timber industry which could lose thousands of jobs if tree cutting is drastically curtailed.

For nearly two decades, environmentalists have fought to preserve the pristine sanctity of the federally owned old-growth forests in Washington and Oregon by trying to force the government to restrict private logging operations. (Roughly 10 percent of old growth is all that remains in the region. The rest has been cut.) The timber industry and many of the elected officials who are its allies argue that any serious reduction in Northwest logging would wreak economic havoc on a regional industry that has been in decline since the 1970s.

An industry lobbying group, the American Forest Resources Alliance, estimates that up to 100,000 people would lose jobs, including thousands of service workers in many depressed rural communities. Some industry critics believe that figure is grossly inflated. But an independent assessment released in July 1991 by four scientists chosen by Congress concluded that as many as 38,000 jobs would be lost in Washington and Oregon.

Several economists who track the timber industry argue that logging cutbacks in the Pacific Northwest would be financially beneficial overall, pointing out that the bulk of the wood supply is produced in southern states and not the Northwest. Thus, they believe, profits would increase by reducing the Northwest lumber supply at a time when a rebounding housing industry may be increasing nationwide demand.

Within the government there is also disagreement over how to resolve the dilemma, not just between Congress and the administration but even between federal agencies. The National Park Service, which runs Olympic National Park where the owls live, has determined that the park is too small to sustain a viable habitat for the owls. The Park Service would like the U.S. Forest Service to restrict logging on its adjoining lands to maintain the owl habitat, but the Forest Service is sensitive to the needs of loggers.

Intramural squabbling is a problem that affects many environmental issues. In the Department of the Interior, the National Park Service generally favors recreational use for federal lands and forests. The Department of Agriculture's U.S. Forest Service advocates a mixed use of logging, recreation, and preservation. The desire of Interior's Bureau of Mines to aid mining interests often clashes with both the Park and Forest services. Likewise, Interior's Bureau of Land Management often conflicts with the Department of Agriculture over the issue of cattle grazing.

The spotted owl, meanwhile, has become the symbol that crystallizes an economic as well as an environmental issue. The Bush Administration says it is looking for a compromise that will serve everyone's interest, but lawsuits have been filed by both the environmentalists and the timber industry. In the end politics—wheeling and dealing—will determine the solution.

The 1990 Clean Air Act is a prime example of politics inducing public policy. Take one aspect of the Act, acid rain. There is significant disagreement within the government and among respected scientists as to the seriousness of the acid-rain problem. Since passage of the $4-billion acid-rain controls statute, the dispute has been given widespread publicity, primarily because of a "60 Minutes" story in early January 1991. The essence of the "60 Minutes" report (and other newspaper and magazine accounts of the controversy, including articles in the *Washington Post* and *Quill*) concerns a 10-year congressionally mandated study of acid rain. Reportedly, the study was virtually ignored by legislators and by the media during the Clean Air Act debate. The study, which cost nearly $540 million and involved approximately 700 of the country's top environmental scientists, generally refuted claims by environmental activists that acid rain was destroying lakes and forests.

A Senate committee spent just one hour listening to testimony about the study and the House never formally received it. It was hardly mentioned by the networks and the major newspapers.

The merits of the study by the National Acid Precipitation Assessment Program (NAPAP) are still being argued, with each side accusing the other of scientific deception. No one can be certain who is right. Even journalists with years of experience covering the environment are ambivalent about the contradictions generated by the controversy. The only certainty is that both sides will continue to present their versions of "scientific evidence."

"There's a lot of good science in the report," says Philip Shabecoff, who was considered one of the premier environmental reporters during 14 years on the beat with the *New York Times*. He left the paper in April 1991 to become executive publisher of a new computer-based daily environmental newsletter, *Greenwire*. "Distinguished scientists on both sides disagree about it. But it should have been given more serious treatment by the media," he says.

Had the media been more diligent in reporting on the NAPAP study, Congress and the administration might have reached a different conclusion concerning the acid rain statute, perhaps saving billions of dollars. Undoubtedly, the publicity would have generated more legislative debate and more public reaction.

It is through the media that politicians gauge public reaction and set public policy, even if that policy is not thoroughly supported by scientific evidence.

"During the debate on the Clean Air Act I was amazed at how much the senators, administrative assistants, and their legislative specialists reacted to the media and the effect the media had on what they did and how they voted," says Ernie Schultz, communications director for Sen. Don Nickles (R-Okla.). Schultz was a news director in Oklahoma City for 16 years and RTNDA's top executive for eight, so he was not naive about how politicians and the media interact. But after a year of observing Congress from the inside he is surprised by the influence and power of the media on the lawmaking process.

"I'd sit in on meetings about the Clean Air Act and experts and scientists would tell us in detail why taking certain steps to reduce air pollution slightly simply wasn't worth the cost in dollars and jobs," Schultz says. "Then the media would do stories that were mostly emotional and had little to do with the facts I had been hearing. And people would start talking about changing their vote.

"The people up here overreact to the media. They read and watch the media as if every voter in their state or district is absorbed by this coverage and is completely taken in by it. Which is ridiculous. But since the first rule of politics is to get elected and the second rule is to get re-elected, the way the issue is presented in the media sometimes becomes more important than reality.

"And the media are much to blame, too, especially on technical and environmental subjects. They go instinctively to the same people for quotes and background, sometimes because the sources have the same ideological bent. You just don't see the same skepticism overall in the media about the environmental-activist side that you do when they're reporting about business and corporate groups. The result is flawed public policy."

It is easy to fault the media for inept coverage of the environment as Schultz does (no matter how constructive his intentions). The media have become the universal scapegoat for most of society's ills. In speaking of the media, however, we are not referring to a monolith but to disparate slices of society comprising thousands of fiefdoms and provinces, some more influential than others.

No one doubts the power of the television networks, weekly news magazines, and major newspapers to help set the nation's agenda. But it is New York and Washington that form the core of media power—and when it comes to reporting on the environment Washington is the heart. Many of the environmental groups active in lobbying are based or have offices there. The politicians who make the laws work there. The corporations which must abide by the laws have their highly paid lobbyists located there. And the bureaucrats who enforce the laws live there.

Of course, in this technological age one need not work in Washington to report effectively on the environment. Most of the best environmental stories on television and radio are done elsewhere. But they almost always have a Washington tie-in. And therein lies the dilemma for anyone covering the environment. The subject is so complex that even Washington-based reporters can find themselves overwhelmed and confused.

Part of the problem is simply the quantity of federal legislation and regulations.

"Federal environmental legislation itself probably runs over a thousand pages," writes James E. Krier, the Earl Warren DeLano Professor of Law at the University of Michigan, and an authority on environmental law and policy:

> The federal regulations implementing the legislation increase that number by an order of magnitude. Many of the regulations are written, literally, in Greek: the alphas, gammas, and deltas used by physical chemists, engineers, and economists. No journalist can hope to become familiar with much of this material, even by faithfully reading secondary sources.
>
> The literature comes from a variety of disciplines, each arcane. The writing is full of jargon and shorthand expressions and buzzes with acronyms: CAA, CWA, CERCLA, SERA, RCRA, TOSCA, NAAQS, NSPS, SIPS, NEPA, EIS, BAT, BDT, RACT, LAER, TECP; each of these refers to legislative programs and provisions administered (in most instances) by—of course—the EPA.
>
> And these are just the *federal* programs and provisions. Over the last 20 years or so the federal government has come to play the dominant role in environmental regulation, but journalists will still have to know about the law at lower levels of government. Most of the federal laws require the states to enact legislation of their own to implement federal mandates, and the states, in turn, have administrative regulations, some of which direct local governments to adopt rules and regulations.[1]

In order to cope with this regulatory complexity and to report accurately and fairly about environmental issues, Professor Krier says journalists must write about the "fundamentally difficult tradeoffs at stake in virtually any environmental controversy."[2]

This is called risk assessment-management whereby the scope and potential danger of a problem is measured against the cost and time required for a solution. (More about risk assessment and risk management in Chapter 3.) Reporters need to remember there are always tradeoffs in assessing risk.

"Which is worse from a public health standpoint?" asks Bud Ward, as an example of a tradeoff one might face in health-based environmental law. "One unit of pollutant for 10 years or 10 units of pollutants for one year?" The answer, of course, affects public policy and the law. And federal environmental laws, stated the EPA's Science Advisory Board in the fall of 1990, "are more reflective of *public perceptions of risk* than of scientific understanding of risk."

If public policy is at the mercy of public perceptions, it may also be at the mercy of the politics of research. That politics is threatening the validity of scientific research should be well understood by journalists who depend on such scholarship to validate a particular opinion or perspective.

Syndicated environmental columnist Warren Brookes believes that because most research is funded by government, the direction and scope of the research is dictated by political agendas.

"A growing share of funding is going to environmental research, which itself is conditional upon the perspective of the researcher, which is to say anti-growth and anti-technology," he writes. "For example, if you are a climatologist who is skeptical of the claims of global warming, you won't get any part of the $1 billion the United States will spend on climate-change research this year (1990). Worse, if you do get the grants and your research fails to support the policy thesis, you face non-renewal, and even difficulty in getting your research published, let alone used."[3]

Brookes cites as one example the aforementioned NAPAP study on acid rain.

Others may disagree with Brookes' perception, but it would be naive to believe that there is no political influence on scientific research. But that political pressure is no more perilous than the manipulation of public opinion by special-interest groups—environmentalists and businesses alike—and by journalists with their own political biases.

Special-Interest Groups

"The environment is too important to be left to the activists and the politicians," James N. Sullivan, vice chairman of the board of the Chevron Corporation, wrote as the decade began.

Sullivan was exhorting his colleagues in the petroleum industry to get more involved in solving environmental problems in order to regain public confidence.

"Public-opinion researchers have found a growing expectation— really, a pent-up demand—for more rigorous government action on a whole range of environmental issues simply because the public doesn't believe we'll do it ourselves," Sullivan continued, citing a 1988 Yankelovich poll commissioned by Chevron. "They don't trust us."[4]

Neither do reporters—and with good reason.

Corporations are, by design, profit-maximizing entities. At times this pursuit of profits has clashed with environmental goals or, in earlier times, taken place without regard for the environment. Some companies have resorted to unconscionable deceptions that later were ferreted out by diligent journalists or angry citizen and environmental groups.

Companies often have hired high-powered public relations firms to deflect journalistic scrutiny and to maneuver public opinion and government action (or inaction). If the business community is suspect, it has itself primarily to blame.

In 1989, the Center for Media and Public Affairs in Washington analyzed all environmental stories appearing on ABC, CBS, and NBC, and in *Time*, *Newsweek*, and *U.S. News and World Report*. According to the survey, big business—particularly oil, agribusiness, and utilities—were blamed 44 percent of the time for creating environmental problems. The U.S. government, in contrast, was cited with 13 percent of the blame.

Even today, as many corporations honestly attempt to atone for past sins, they often are met with skepticism and ridicule, even by the least-belligerent environmentalists.

When asked about the oil industry's recent environmental efforts, such as encouraging the recycling of motor oil and the development of cleaner-burning gasoline, Michael Francis of the Wilderness Society told the *Washington Post*: "My gut tells me it's more image than anything. They're trying to sound green, but really, are they green on the interior?"[5]

Bob Hattoway of the Sierra Club told the *Post*: "We had the oil companies oppose the Clean Air Act, the double-hulled tanker provisions, the fuel efficiency and mileage-standard improvements...and any controls on their price gouging of the American consumers. So, quite simply, we just don't believe them."[6]

Some journalists have the same suspicions. And that's okay. It should be a fundamental part of the journalistic creed to be skeptical.

But if journalists are going to continue to scrutinize and question the motives of big business—and well they should—they must also be wary and skeptical of other special-interest groups, particularly the environmentalists.

Reporters and news directors need to comprehend the political leanings, philosophies, and agendas of environmental groups to understand why they do what they do, and to judge equitably the merits of their claims. This learning process is also a way to avoid being deluded, deceived, and manipulated by the unscrupulous and the zealous. Even the most experienced journalists sometimes have difficulty penetrating the infrastructure of the environmental movement.

Dave Ropeik of WCVB-TV in Boston is one of a small cadre of full-time environmental reporters in local television. "As I look back on my environmental reporting," he says, "the one, single major mistake I made was taking the environmentalists' word as gospel. I didn't challenge them as I challenged the other side and that cost me dearly. I oversimplified or gave the wrong impression."

Like the media, environmentalists are not monolithic. There are more than 10,000 environmental and conservation organizations in the United States, each with its own agenda. Frequently they work together. Sometimes they work against each other. Factions within organizations often clash and it is not uncommon to find politics—personal and social—at the root of a public dispute.

"Overall, the environmental movement in a broad sense has very similar goals," says Phil Kavits, senior director of radio and television for the National Wildlife Federation, "but we are different in the tactics and approach to specific issues."

"Environmental organizations are not alike," says Eric Swanson, who spent 12 years in the environmental field before becoming executive director of the Radio and Television News Directors Foundation. "They vary greatly in mission and scope, and range from the very conservative to the very liberal. However, all vie for and use media coverage to achieve their goals."

Swanson classifies the groups into five very broad categories, though he admits it is an oversimplified sketch. His five general "camps" are:

- Advocacy and Legal Action—Groups such as the Natural Resources Defense Council, Sierra Club, and the Wilderness Society that are involved in lobbying and legal action affecting state and federal policies.
- Public Education and Policy Research—Groups such as the National Wildlife Federation, the National Audubon Society, and the Conservation Foundation/World Wildlife Fund which get involved in policy primarily through research and public information.
- Outdoor Recreation—Groups with large sportsman constituencies, such as the Izaak Walton League and Ducks Unlimited, that want to protect hunting habitats and species.
- Land Conservation—Groups like the Nature Conservancy, the Conservation Fund, and hundreds of land trusts that purchase land for preservation; these groups are typically more conservative, quiet, and garner little media attention.
- Local Citizens—A "catch all" for the thousands of local groups that are active in everything from neighborhood recycling campaigns to the local siting of hazardous waste facilities.

"Often the groups cross over," Swanson says. "For example, the National Wildlife Federation, which is primarily involved in research and education, is also heavily involved in advocacy and outdoor recreation. But the real action and the bulk of activity is in the last category. This is where the best and worst examples of media coverage might occur, as these citizen groups can be very visible and easily attract local media attention. If the group is poorly funded, has done inadequate research, is under pressure, or is emotional or irresponsible, the media coverage can be flawed unless the journalist can ferret out the facts."

Swanson's classification might be expanded to include a separate category for activist organizations whose tactics range from trespassing and harassment (such as Greenpeace) to property destruction and outright violence (such as Earth First). Such groups are considered to be on the radical end of the environmental spectrum, and seem to attract a disproportionate amount of media attention for their provocative actions.

Outside Magazine, which monitors the environment primarily from a recreational perspective, analyzed 25 prominent environmental organizations in its September 1990 issue. It looked at philosophy, leadership, programs, and funding, and ranked the organizations by their volatility and aggressiveness. Earth First (which cuts down power lines and threatens violence against loggers by hiding spikes in trees) and the Sea Shepherd Conservation Society (which sinks whaling ships and robs seal hunters) were rated the most radical and cited as "bomb-throwers." The National Wildlife Federation and Ducks Unlimited were rated least extremist and labeled "milquetoasts."

Outside criticized some environmental groups for becoming too cozy with corporations—accepting funding it considered questionable if not a conflict of interest, for example, and reproached them for creating bureaucracies, publicity machines, and executive perks that sometimes rivaled those of companies on the "other side."

"*Outside* totally distorted facts while glossing over the good," says Kavits of the National Wildlife Federation (NWF), which was one of the organizations criticized. "You must remember that the editors had their own agenda, and that we're a natural target for them because the NWF is the largest organization with the biggest budget."

It was another organization, however, that was cited most frequently as an environmental source by the networks and newsmagazines, according to the Center for Media and Public Affairs' 1989 study of environmental stories. That distinction went to the Natural Resources Defense Council (NRDC), probably because of its role in perpetrating the Alar pesticide apple scare in February 1989. Inside the environmental movement, the NRDC generally is respected as a solid, astute organization that uses science and the law in an aggressive manner to achieve its activist goals. But in the Alar escapade, it went too far.

The NRDC charged that Alar, a chemical sprayed on apples, posed a major cancer risk—particularly for children who consume large amounts of apples and apple products. The NRDC allowed "60 Minutes" to break the story exclusively, which it did in a segment anchored by Ed Bradley on February 26, 1989.

The next day, the NRDC held well-attended news conferences in New York, Washington, and 12 other cities to release its report "Intolerable risk: Pesticides in our children's food." A week later, actress Meryl Streep told a Washington news conference she was helping to form the NRDC's "Mothers and Others for Pesticide Limits." The media blitz was on. Hundreds of stories in national and local media followed.

Despite assurances by the Alar manufacturer, apple growers, other scientists, and three government agencies—the EPA, the Department of Agriculture, and the Food and Drug Administration—the nation panicked. Wholesale and retail sales of apples temporarily plunged. School districts pulled apples from lunchrooms. Grocers advertised sales of "Alar-free" apples. Eventually, the manufacturer voluntarily took Alar off the market. The EPA banned the pesticide in May 1990 even though the science behind that move has been questioned.

In the Fall 1990 *Issues in Science and Technology*, the official journal of the National Academy of Sciences, Dr. Joseph Rosen, a professor of food science at Rutgers University, wrote that there was never a "legitimate scientific study to justify the Alar scare." He dissected in detail the history of the scientific tests dating back to the early 1970s and called what the NRDC did "irresponsible."[7] The NRDC claims it simply wished to point out the dangers of pesticides. But the NRDC did misuse EPA figures. In fact Alar was used on just 6 percent of the existing apple crop at the time—but the NRDC didn't mention that during its hyped-up media campaign.

Ultimately, stories began appearing here and there denouncing the media for exaggerating the story. But negative perceptions generated by such enormous publicity are always difficult to overcome. Meanwhile "60 Minutes" continues to stand behind its broadcast. "We believe the broadcast highlighted an important public health matter," a CBS spokesman told the Associated Press when 11 Washington apple growers filed suit against the NRDC on November 29, 1990. "It was well researched and well documented."

The NRDC has not backed away either. A day after the suit was filed, Janet Hathaway, the NRDC lawyer who authored the report, told the *New York Times*: "We definitely made the apple industry think. The industry is now interested in reducing its pesticide use."

To orchestrate its Alar crusade the NRDC hired a professional public relations firm, Fenton Communications. Two months into the media campaign, owner David Fenton bragged about his success in a long memorandum that later found its way into the *Wall Street Journal*:

> Our goal was to create so many repetitions of NRDC's message that average American consumers (not just the policy elite in Washington) could not avoid hearing it—from many different media outlets within a short period of time. The idea was for the "story" to achieve a life of its own, and continue for weeks and months to affect policy and consumer habits....In most regards, this goal was met....[8]

In retrospect, the Alar scare tarnished both the environmentalists and the media. "It absolutely backfired," says Phil Kavits of the NWF. "There were some poor calls in handling it by the NRDC. But it also turned into a media feeding frenzy."

If the media are to avoid future feeding frenzies, they must be more skeptical of the scientific claims of environmental groups, more aware of their political nature, and more attentive to the rigidity of their philosophies. Journalists also need to be wary of how these groups describe themselves. Labels such as "public-interest," "consumer," and "pro-environment" are fatuous and nebulous. (The same warning, of course, should apply to the recent spate of "green" and "pro-environment" claims being made by corporations.) Reporters also must be knowledgeable about the background of the groups—their leadership, membership, and financial support—if they are to assess the merits of their assertions.

The groups should be identified on the air by their political and social ties. Who funds them may be crucial to public understanding of what they are advocating.

Unless journalists are vigilant about all special-interest groups—environmentalists and corporations alike—it is quite simple for a handful of individuals to band together, call themselves a "public-interest, pro-environment consumer organization," and entice the media to a high-profile news conference in Washington with some dire warning about global warming. Or higher consumer costs. Or pesticides in apples.

Journalists covering the environment might take to heart a somewhat wistful observation by author Bill Gifford in his *Outside* article on environmental organizations: "If only there weren't so many groups, and if only they weren't so susceptible to the usual foibles of business and human nature."[9]

Advocacy Journalism

Perhaps the biggest challenge for the local radio or television station covering the environment is whether to take an advocacy position. This does not mean that one advocates for clean air or against hazardous wastes. As many pundits have said, how can anyone be *against* clean air and *for* hazardous wastes?

No, environmental advocacy in the broadest sense means presenting a particular point of view to the exclusion of others or offering a specific solution to a problem. Advocacy journalism means different things to different people. Thus, defining what we mean by "advocacy" is vital to understanding why some respected journalists favor a measure of advocacy and others abhor it entirely.

In its most extreme definition, advocacy means endorsing a position with little or no objectivity, fairness, or balance, and disregarding or denigrating information that conflicts with the chosen position.

At the other end of the spectrum, advocacy can be defined less contentiously as the presentation of a conclusion or opinion *after* conflicting arguments have been fairly presented.

"Certainly I believe advocacy is justified," says ABC's Roger Caras, "but not blind advocacy. After more than 30 years, people certainly know I'm coming from a definite position. So, I'm an advocate. But I also believe in being fair at all times or my credibility will suffer."

The key words in any discussion of advocacy are the traditional journalistic tenets of objectivity, balance, and fairness. Many journalists argue that one can never be truly objective. Nor, many assert, should one always seek to maintain balance. Especially when reporting on science, the principle of balance may give undue weight to a minor or discredited view.

But only the most radical advocacy journalist excludes fairness— and it is the issue of fairness that is the quintessence of the advocacy debate. Fairness, of course, often is in the mind of the beholder. What is fair to one side may not seem fair to the other simply because of their polarized agendas, beliefs, and opinions.

Two print journalists, Mark Hertsgaard and Warren Brookes, may best epitomize this polarization. Hertsgaard is a contributing editor of *Rolling Stone* who makes no effort to hide his liberal, Democratic, anti-business philosophy and invariably blames Republican leaders and corporations for fouling up the environment. Brookes is a *Detroit News* columnist whose work is syndicated by Creators Syndicate to 60 newspapers, including the conservative *Washington Times*. Brookes has gained prominence (or perhaps notoriety) by refuting some of the cherished tenets of the environmental activists.

Although there are other journalists who foster and actively endorse specific environmentally liberal points of view—notably those at

Turner Broadcasting Inc. and Time-Warner Corporation—Hertsgaard is one of the most openly biased.

In a November 1989 *Rolling Stone* article ridiculing President Bush's environmental concepts and chastising the media for not being stronger advocates, Hertsgaard wrote:

"But as central pillars of the American establishment themselves, the nation's leading news organizations are decidedly unreceptive to ideas challenging capitalist orthodoxy. Nor do they tend to do much tough coverage of their fellow corporate giants....In any case, the press has the obligation to illuminate the dimensions and roots of the environmental crisis and identify and analyze potential solutions."[10]

Of course, what is an environmental crisis and solution to Hertsgaard may not be to Brookes. Now based in Washington, Brookes has challenged just about every environmental issue from clean air to radon. That has earned him the wrath of many environmentalists, politicians, and other journalists who believe he is a corporate apologist or even an insincere sensationalist.

"He certainly takes a more pro-industry stance than environmentalists feel is appropriate," says Allan Margolin, media director for the Environmental Defense Fund and a former ABC news producer. "But one has to remember columnists have axes to grind."

"Warren never met a pollutant he couldn't defend," says Bud Ward, who has mixed feelings about Brookes. "One of these days, he will have to find an environmental issue he likes."

Still, Brookes' approach merits attention because he typically presents data that counter the prevailing theories espoused by activists and journalistic advocates such as Hertsgaard. A pivotal series of Brookes' columns in August 1989, for example, debunked an ABC-TV series on acid rain and led to a *Forbes* cover story discrediting theories on global warming.

Phil Kavits, who was a television reporter for nearly a decade before becoming an executive with the National Wildlife Federation, warns that extreme advocates on both sides may harm their credibility.

"There is a fundamental rightness to the environmental goal and we all believe in that," he says. "But those who immerse themselves so thoroughly sometimes run the risk of getting on a soap box and they become zealots. They may take a point of view but they should be fair."

And thus we return full circle to the meaning of fairness. Perhaps there is no better way for a reporter to practice fairness than to follow the dictionary definition: "...free from favor toward either or any side. *Fair* implies an elimination of personal feelings, interests, or prejudices so as to achieve a proper balance of conflicting needs, rights, or demands...."

Advocacy—especially the extreme advocacy that has little use for the dictionary definition of fairness—seems to occur more frequently in print than in electronic journalism. Rarely is there extreme advocacy in local TV news. Local TV news strives for fairness and balance more than any other medium. Some would suggest this is due in part to intimidation by government regulators. But the networks, including the Public Broadcasting Service (PBS) and cable networks, seem less inhibited about advocating particular points of view, especially on environmental issues.

That was discussed fervently in the fall of 1989 at a major environmental symposium in Washington sponsored by the Smithsonian Institution and co-chaired by the CEOs of ABC, CBS, NBC, and Turner Broadcasting, among others. Several speakers talked of advocacy at the networks, including NBC's Andrea Mitchell who then covered Congress and, thus, the legislative process that determines public policy about the environment.

Another speaker was Barbara Pyle, environmental editor for Turner Broadcasting System, who admits that she quit being an "objective journalist" years ago. Her boss, Ted Turner, is an avowed environmentalist and makes no apology for being an advocate. To some degree, neither do many of those who work for him. Turner and others devoutly believe the global problems of the environment are so urgent, so immense, and so potentially catastrophic to mankind that often traditional journalism is ineffectual.

"We are running out of time," says Barbara Pyle. But even Turner's advocates say they can be fair, though maybe not in the traditional journalistic sense.

Teya Ryan is a senior producer for Turner's "Network Earth" series and a vice president of the new Society of Environmental Journalists. In the Summer 1990 issue of the *Gannett Center Journal* which was devoted to "Covering the environment," Ryan wrote:

> The creed of a "balanced perspective" has been the hallmark of journalism for the past 30 years. But I wonder if it isn't time in the 1990s for a different kind of reporting, a different kind of presentation to the public, one that says simply: "This is what I saw as a reporter. This is whom I talked to. This is my perspective, and here are my suggestions for change. If you want another point of view, find it from another broadcaster or newspaper."
>
> ...I would never assume that by being an advocate a journalist is absolved from following the common guidelines of fairness. Your facts must be secure, and you must be ready to defend them. Neither does advocacy lessen the quality of the report or the journalist. Remember Edward R. Murrow's "Harvest of Shame"? But advocacy does mean that reporters take a more personal point of view. It may not be balance, but it is quality journalism.[11]

ABC's Roger Caras argues that basic journalistic rules do not apply to every story and that sometimes a reporter cannot avoid a point of view. But, he insists, fairness still is imperative.

"Always give the other side a fair turn," he says. "Don't edit them so it appears to be something they didn't say. Let them say it or don't use it at all."

Some advocates believe it is wrong for reporters to be simply stenographers, reporting on every side of an issue and giving equal balance to each position, no matter how minor or trivial the viewpoint. Like Charles Alexander, a senior editor at *Time* magazine and a crusader for environmental advocacy, they insist there must be analysis and interpretation.

However, another SEJ board member who also believes in advocacy admits there is danger in such decision making. In the Winter 1990-91 edition of the *SEJournal,* Tom Meersman of Minnesota Public Radio wrote: "The debate about advocacy in journalism seems to center on this point. When should a reporter simply present opposing arguments, and when should he or she feel confident enough to take the story a step further...to suggest which of the claims seem to have more merit?"[12]

Mark Hertsgaard believes journalists must "prescribe solutions."

Dave Ropeik of WCVB-TV in Boston does not consider himself an advocacy journalist but believes reporters should draw conclusions. "I believe it is my journalistic duty to make a judgment on behalf of the viewer based on the facts and scientific information I gather," he says. "I will use my expertise to determine who I think is right or wrong and who is telling the truth or not, and I will tell that to the viewer."

But there are some who believe reporters who interpret and make judgments are flirting precariously with the public's trust. S. Robert Lichter, co-director of the Center for Media and Public Affairs, says journalists have traditionally seen themselves as advocates of social change in America. But until the late 1960s, the media also had been traditionally objective, he notes. "Now they are taking sides," he says, "and this is fraught with danger.

"In the last 20 years the media have moved away from the dispassionate approach of the past. The old model was like Joe Friday—'just the facts ma'am.' The new model is to be like Robin Hood, taking information from the rich and giving to the poor. The media have become more political. The danger is they are losing their credibility with the public."

The traditionalists' view is best summed up by Jim Detjen, the first president of SEJ, who has won several awards for his environmental reporting for the *Philadelphia Inquirer.* In the *Gannett Center Journal* he wrote:

> I believe that advocacy journalism, if it means one-sided and unfair reporting, is misguided and in the long run counterproductive. If major newspapers, magazines, and broadcast stations adopt an advocacy philosophy, the media will be

treading on dangerous ground that could alienate readers and viewers and cause them to stop trusting the media. Journalists who have spent their careers establishing reputations for fairness and accuracy could suddenly find their credibility evaporating.

Readers [and viewers] have a right to expect that the media are performing their responsibilities fairly and without bias. Since the public does not know whether or not the media are, in fact, reporting the news objectively, they must trust the stewards of the institution to ensure those who write and edit the news are not improperly influenced by financial, ideological, or other personal considerations.[13]

If more reporters and news directors concerned with environmental coverage abided by Detjen's philosophy, there might be less acrimony and less mistrust among us all—and maybe even better public policy.

II. Television and Radio News and the Environment

No one doubts the power of television news. In mere seconds, an event can be transformed from an obscure, provincial happening in some remote corner of the world into an international incident with far-reaching repercussions. Radio news has its own niche, providing fast updates of breaking stories. But TV news simply has extraordinary influence—and therein lies its major strength and weakness.

It is the reason television usually bears the brunt of criticism whenever the media's environmental coverage is analyzed. For TV news, while it has the ability to influence masses and create perceptions, can also oversimplify complex issues. And when the subject is an environmental problem with all its scientific and technical intricacies, TV news coverage often is inadequate.

Even today, there are only a handful of full-time environmental reporters in local TV news, and too often what passes for environmental coverage at many stations is simply crisis reporting of a breaking news event—a coastal oil spill, the clean-up of a hazardous waste site, an overturned tanker leaking poisonous fumes. In a 1991 nationwide survey conducted by the Radio and Television News Directors Foundation, only 26 percent of 102 television and radio news directors responding claimed to have a full-time environmental reporter. About three-quarters (76 percent) said they regularly assign environmental stories to general-assignment reporters, weekend anchors, or meteorologists.

In-depth, ongoing reporting on serious scientific and health environmental issues has not been widespread in local television. Contrast this with the print medium where many newspaper reporters have been assigned full time to the environmental beat for 10 to 20 years.

One cannot deny that television news (and especially local TV news) has many faults and inherent weaknesses. But to blame it for all the ills of environmental journalism is to be myopic and often overly critical.

TV news does have pressures and idiosyncrasies that are unique to the medium. It must compete intensely for viewers, not only against news rivals (in various media) but also against multifarious entertainment attractions. It is graphic, emotional, and fleeting. Yet it is these very characteristics that infuse TV news with the power to shape public perceptions so forcefully. The impact of television coverage of the Persian Gulf War proved that most dramatically.

However, TV news as we know it in 1991 is already an anachronism. Cable News Network may be king of the hill—for now. Yet in this age of satellites, lightweight portable electronic equipment, computers, and instant world-wide communication, no one can predict what the news business will look like by the end of the century. Already, the other three U.S. networks are forming alliances with communications groups in Japan, England, and elsewhere to compete for the international audience. The advent in the United States of direct broadcast satellites (DBS)—already a reality in several countries—could personalize the delivery of news into individual homes, with unpredictable repercussions on public perceptions. And the continued development of fiber optics and digital technology will most certainly affect the production and dissemination of news.

Local TV news also is continuing to evolve. Traditional newscasts remain prominent at the dinner hour and late at night. But local news can now be found virtually around the clock in many cities.

Independent-station newscasts have proliferated. Over-the-air broadcasters have formed partnerships with other broadcasters or cable operators to produce newscasts, sometimes in competition with themselves. Cable entities are originating local news in Long Island, N.Y., Orange County, Calif., and elsewhere. Local newscasts delivered through DBS and fiber optics are also on the horizon and may one day revolutionize local news delivery. However, some observers predict the termination of news at many stations within 10 years. And there have been increasingly frequent rumblings that one or more of the three broadcast networks may radically downsize or even dismantle their news operations.

Radio news could also change, but more in response to market pressures than technological advancements. All-news radio stations will thrive in major metropolitan areas, and some music and talk stations will continue to stress a news presence in their towns and cities. Public radio will be there for selected listeners, and a handful of networks will continue delivering newscasts and soundbites to affiliates and subscribers.

There is one certainty. Local radio and TV news in some form or another will flourish. And since both the public and politicians believe the environment is a prime issue of the 1990s, local radio and TV news should be at the forefront in reporting, examining, and analyzing environmental matters.

News directors need to develop and support environmental specialists—reporting and producing teams whenever feasible—rather than merely exploit the credibility of weathermen in part-time environmental roles. General-assignment reporters, newscast producers, and assignment editors need to become familiar with the basic environmental terminology, politics, and issues in order to prevent manipulation, avoid distortions, and maintain credibility.

And everyone in radio and television news would do well to reflect on environmental coverage of the past and to study the present so that a better job might be done in the future.

Crisis Coverage

Covering a breaking story in a crisis is the heart of television and radio news. At one time this was the domain of radio. But today, with its capability to go "live" instantaneously from virtually anywhere in the world, television is the medium of choice.

Radio can still have impact. It can update quickly and reinforce the essence of a story, particularly when reporting on a crisis of national interest. But its on-the-scene coverage has diminished at both the network and local levels. Many radio stations have eliminated news departments entirely; even at the larger operations, the role of the street reporter has given way to the anchor who relies on a telephone to chase down leads and talk to newsmakers.

Long before satellites and microwave equipment, television forced radio news into the background. During the 1960s and 1970s, dramatic pictures of the civil rights movement and the Vietnam war demonstrated the breadth of TV's power but also the depth of its faults. In covering a crisis, TV news is most deleterious and most vulnerable. For in its coverage, whether taped or "live," TV news can make an event into something different than it really is.

TV news is an emotional medium. Participants get emotionally involved in an event and so does the audience watching it on the screen. Emotions tend to simplify or even distort.

During a crisis, the ebb and flow of emotions hardens public perceptions. And no matter what corrective efforts are attempted later, the initial perception is not easily altered. This is what often happens during the reporting of an environmental crisis on television—and why TV news is so susceptible to manipulation by people and organizations that exploit emotions.

Perhaps there is no better example than the reporting of the nuclear reactor meltdown at Three Mile Island in 1979. Three Mile Island was a milestone in environmental crisis reporting and a watershed for television news.

To this day, much of the public believes the nation was teetering on the edge of a nuclear disaster of cataclysmic proportions in March and April of 1979, and that radiation leaks from the plant caused nearby residents to develop cancer in later years. It is a controversy that endures.

Academicians such as Robert DuPont have suggested that the public's fear of nuclear power was heightened significantly by the media's confusing and sometimes sensational reporting from Three Mile Island (and from Chernobyl in 1986). Certainly the nuclear accident near Harrisburg, Pa., was serious; a potentially explosive hydrogen bubble within the plant posed a real threat until it was vented. But the actual danger may have been exaggerated at the time by a combination of television news hyperbole, industry misstatements, and government bungling.

Journalists covering Three Mile Island had little or no understanding of nuclear energy and nuclear power plants. They showed up as reporters on a breaking news story, and the complexities and technicalities of the circumstance were beyond their comprehension. Their stories were often based more on emotion than facts.

Ed Wickenheiser, then the news director at radio station WSBA in York, Pa., was the first journalist on the scene.

"The people in the area had lived in the shadow of two nuclear plants for years so there wasn't much concern at first," he recalls. "A couple of newspaper people showed up and then some local TV guys and the next day the out-of-towners began coming in and it was like an Army arriving. In the beginning, we all used one telephone booth outside the plant and our two-way radios. Communications was poor. Remember, this was before computers, so the telephone was the main link for reporting. It wasn't until three days later that a battery of telephones was installed.

"With the exception of the *New York Times* reporter, no one had a specialty in this and the terminology was basically Greek to everyone. We really didn't know what we were reporting or what questions to ask."

"It was very confusing in the first few days," admits Kelly Burke, then a reporter for Washington's WRC-TV. "The power company and government officials weren't very organized and they were downplaying the accident. The residents were very laid back and supportive of the Three Mile Island owners. So, when we started to hear about a possible meltdown, it was a little scary. We really didn't know what that meant. When we tried to ask the people in charge, they either wouldn't make themselves available or they would downplay it. We were pretty much on our own."

As the story unfolded, emotions rather than science fed the public psyche. A harried Walter Cronkite told his CBS audience that they were seeing a "nuclear nightmare." Ralph Nader, an anti-nuclear-power activist, hustled before the cameras to proclaim: "All the public needs to know is that there is radiation in the nuclear power plant and it's a thousand times more radioactive than the blast at Hiroshima!"

"Some media overdid it," says Wickenheiser, now the news director at WGAL-TV in nearby Lancaster, Pa. "The farther from the scene, the bigger and bolder the headlines. I remember seeing out-of-town headlines about 'mass evacuations' which did not happen and the report of a German news team in particular that claimed a half block in Middletown was starting to radiate. We all kinda joked about that, wondering when we were going to start glowing."

Later that year, a task force looking into media coverage of the accident said the media's specific handling of radiation information was "abysmally inadequate." The Task Force on the Public's Right to Information, a committee of the President's Commission on the Accident at Three Mile Island (or "Kemeny Commission"), charged that reporters did not give sufficient background information and made improper comparisons and factually impossible statements.

Sharon Friedman, chairperson of the journalism department at Lehigh University where she also directs one of the country's few science and environmental writing programs, was a consultant to the task force.

"It wasn't so much that the media overplayed the story," she says, "but that they reported out of context, giving the wrong impression. Yes, there was some sensational reporting and some newspapers were as guilty as television. But it wasn't all the media's fault. They were confused. The engineers on the scene did not help as they should have. So, the media used sources that were abysmal."

Aside from the media coverage, the cancer issue is still being debated. Some TMI residents believe radiation from the accident has been a significant cause of cancer, and three reporters who covered the story have died from cancer since 1985. Tony Mauro of *USA Today* and Gannett News Service believes he may have developed Hodgkin's Disease at TMI but admits he has no scientific proof. In fact, one major authority on the TMI cancer question says there is no basis for any claim of an increase in cancer or birth defects. Dr. Kenneth Miller, head of radiology at the Hershey Medical Center, reached that conclusion after studying TMI residents for 10 years.

Though Three Mile Island became the nadir of the U.S. nuclear power industry, it was a different milestone for local TV news. At the time, local news was expanding rapidly throughout the country. Staffs were increasing. Newscasts were being added. Equipment was being upgraded with emphasis on the new "live" microwave technology to widen the traditional coverage area.

Because of its close proximity to the major population centers of New York, Washington, Baltimore, Philadelphia, and Pittsburgh, Three Mile Island was inundated with local TV crews from the East and Midwest. The three networks were there in force for their nightly newscasts and morning talk shows but now they had to make room for their local affiliates and several independents.

Portable satellite dishes were not in widespread use so there was little live reporting from the plant site. But local reporters were sending personalized stories back home every day, supplementing the dire network coverage and, by just being there, magnifying the real or imagined gravity of the crisis for their viewers.

One can only speculate on public perceptions—and hysteria—had dozens of local stations and CNN converged on Three Mile Island to report "live" around-the-clock as they would today. Live reporting accentuates the emotional aspects of a crisis; thus, it is not difficult to envision the panic that might have ensued because of irresponsible "live" reports from uninformed and unprepared local TV journalists.

No environmental crisis has mesmerized local and network TV news as Three Mile Island did. The chemical disaster at Bhopal, India, the nuclear accident at Chernobyl, and the Kuwait oil fires became international incidents and were well covered by the networks. So were the Valdez oil spill in Prince William Sound and the fires in Yellowstone National Park. Though local newscasts carried network excerpts on those stories, few local stations sent crews to Russia, Alaska, or Wyoming to do stories for themselves. A new austerity in newsroom budgets had taken its toll on travel by the late 1980s—and anyway, there were plenty of environmental crises at home to keep reporters busy.

Toxic chemical spills from overturned railroad cars and tanker trucks. Excess pollution from industrial waste in rivers and lakes. Overflowing landfills. Garbage and medical waste washing up on beaches. Oil storage fires. They've all been part of the day-to-day coverage of breaking stories on local TV newscasts.

Some have even won national accolades. One memorable example was a 1989 railroad car fire near Dayton, Ohio, which won WHIO-TV an international RTNDA award for spot news. It is featured in college journalism textbooks as the definitive illustration of live-action reporting of a crisis event.

But one problem in covering a local crisis is the difficulty of keeping the event in perspective. The discovery of certain pollutants in a lake, for instance, may alarm local residents. But in the overall scheme of environmental quandaries, the health risks of a polluted lake may be minimal when measured against such potentially catastrophic issues as global warming and deforestation. However, it's difficult for journalists and viewers to become interested in problems like ozone depletion and soil erosion when there is no evidence of a crisis at hand, no smoking railroad tanker or oozing lake sludge to see.

When it comes to the environment, journalists and viewers tend to be much more interested in what's happening in their own backyard than in what's occurring thousands of miles away. They're more concerned with what's in their backyard today than what might be there a dozen years from now. And they're more absorbed by what is perceived to be a dangerous reality—such as hazardous waste—than by a threatening but vague dilemma like global warming.

As a result of this parochial approach, the public overreacts to some environmental problems and underestimates others. Likewise, politicians and public policies often veer off on tangents from more consequential environmental issues. And journalists frequently mislead themselves and their audiences.

Love Canal epitomizes what can happen when scientific uncertainty collides with media gullibility. Love Canal became a national symbol of chemical waste disposal in the late 1970s and early 1980s. The Hooker Chemical Company had dumped wastes, including the chemical dioxin, into an unused canal near Niagara Falls for 10 years before filling in the site in the 1950s and selling it to the school board. A community was built on the old dumping site. Years later residents started complaining about chemicals seeping into their basements and problems with the drinking water.

The local newspaper began publishing stories about the neighborhood's chemical problems and soon Buffalo-area radio and TV stations were onto the story. A state investigation ensued. The school was closed. Residents were evacuated. And the national media spread the story from coast to coast.

If it could happen at Love Canal it could happen anywhere, the media reasoned. Some local TV stations and newspapers sent reporters to Love Canal to see for themselves—and they returned home to look for chemical problems in *their* neighborhoods. In a short time hundreds of other toxic dumps were reported throughout the United States. Love Canal had become a symbol for government callousness and corporate negligence.

Although the health risk at Love Canal was real, debate continued on the extent of the danger. Scientific evidence proved contradictory and confusion mounted within the Environmental Protection Agency (EPA). Many in the media, uninformed about the complexities of science and the environment, did an inadequate job of explaining all of this to their audiences. They jumped to the wrong conclusions and took a scared public with them.

Some observers believe Love Canal was too much of a media event because of reporters' herd instinct that spawned spurious stories of toxic wastes around the country. The media have been blamed for causing unnecessary fear and overreaction as they were blamed at Three Mile Island.

But Rae Tyson, who covered Love Canal for the *Niagara Gazette* and now reports on the environment for *USA Today*, believes a larger issue was the evaluation of scientific information. "I am convinced the danger at Love Canal was real," he says. "But the uncertainty of science in assessing the risk was as true there as it has been at every other environmental disaster."

Tyson's point about scientific contradictions is even more significant now that the EPA has admitted that the dangers of the chemical compound dioxin were exaggerated. The EPA is conducting a yearlong review on the risks of dioxin but scientists who originally determined dioxin was so hazardous now say they were wrong. Toxins more threatening than dioxin caused the actual health risk at Love Canal. But still the science was imperfect and those who lived in Love Canal made sure the media knew it.

"There was some manipulation of the scientific information by the residents, particularly with the second evacuation in 1980," Tyson says. "This got to be very emotional but you have to remember these were desperate people. Sometimes the emotions, rather than the science, became the story. This was particularly true for out-of-town media, print and electronic, which failed to understand the history and complexities of the problem."

Emotion and science. When it comes to environmental reporting of crisis events there is probably too much of one and not enough of the other—especially in television news.

TV's Environmental Journalists

When Joyce Reid was the news director at KYTV in Springfield, Mo., in the early 1980s, a young general-assignment reporter named Erin Hayes approached her about a story on toxic wastes.

Hayes was from Eureka Springs, Ark., a small town in the nearby Ozarks. She was concerned about the dumping of chemical wastes in her hometown area and believed something should be done about it.

Reid agreed to give Hayes time to develop the story, and within a few days the young woman's reports began appearing on the early and late newscasts. Night after night, Hayes told viewers in the nation's 88th market about the problem of dioxin and other chemicals. Soon, she was reporting on other landfills and air pollution and after a few months Reid assigned Hayes to cover the environment full time.

"It took about three years for Erin to establish herself with the viewers and the industry," recalls Reid, "and she was finally recognized for her contributions in state, regional, and national contests. Columbia-DuPont gave her a couple of awards.

"I made the commitment to Erin to cover the environment when hardly anyone else was doing it. I had the support of the general manager and it paid off. But it wasn't easy."

Joyce Reid and Erin Hayes are no longer in Springfield and the station's environmental reporting has been reduced. But Reid and Hayes' commitment to environmental journalism has not diminished.

Hayes is now a general-assignment reporter for CBS based in Atlanta and continues to do environmental stories whenever she can. Reid is news director at KDBC-TV in El Paso. Her passion for environmental reporting is restrained only by her budgetary limitations.

"In my priorities, covering the environment is right behind the day-to-day coverage of breaking news," she says. "Although El Paso is now the 22nd largest city in the United States, this is a small ADI, the 100th market, and we just don't have the resources that are available in bigger markets. But we have every environmental problem you can imagine: air pollution, nuclear-waste dumping, contaminated water. I'd like to do more coverage of the environment but I just don't have the staff to assign someone full time."

Neither Reid nor Hayes are familiar names in the world of environmental journalism, but they may be symbolic of local TV news and environmental reporting. They work in an ephemeral medium with little history for reporting on anything but breaking environmental crises; and, they earned their environmental reputations in small television markets, far from the country's media centers. For years, they worked in obscurity and now, in this era of downsizing, they must give way to other coverage priorities that take precedence over the environment.

Many newspaper journalists have been covering the environment as a full-time or part-time beat for 20 years so it is natural for those reporters to be better known. They know each other, having shared information and ideas, and they're well known by their sources in government and environmental organizations.

Even at the networks, there are not many reporters assigned full time to the environment. An exception is CNN where environmental commitment is part of Ted Turner's corporate philosophy. Of the other three networks, ABC appears to have the most commitment. In addition to Roger Caras's wildlife beat, the environment is now a regular part of ABC's *World News Tonight*—Barry Serafin and Ned Potter are assigned full time to report for the "American Agenda" segment.

Local TV news has never fully adopted the beat system and only in the last few years have some TV reporters specialized in science, health, or the environment. But unless their work is seen regularly on the network or through syndication, they are practically unknown to each other. Nor are they well known to government sources and environmental groups outside their market or region.

Undoubtedly, there are others like Reid and Hayes who have covered, or are now covering, the environment full time or part time for local television—perhaps many more than critics realize.

Kim Standish tracks local TV news for her weekly insider newsletter *The Rundown*. Over the years she has cited several stations for their exemplary environmental coverage. KRON-TV in San Francisco, WRAL-TV in Raleigh, and WCVB-TV in Boston are among them. All three have management commitment to some degree but approach the coverage differently.

At KRON-TV, Dr. Tom Linden is assigned to the health and environment beat, but it is Target 4 reporter/producer Greg Lyon who sometimes takes the station lead with his investigative series and background reports. Associate news director Ian Pearson coordinates coverage from his special-projects unit and sometimes uses the weather people. There is no regular environmental segment in the KRON-TV newscasts but sometimes environment is the lead. Series are often used on both the early and late news. Subject matter ranges from hard news—like the multi-part toxic waste series—to soft.

"As the general manager," says Amy McCombs, "it is my job to raise the consciousness of the station on what we should focus on. Covering the environment is part of the overall fabric of this station. In going through the thought process of their jobs I want all employees to think about what we can do toward that end."

WRAL-TV weekend anchor Bill Leslie covers the environment during the week. But the station's programming department gets deeply involved in year-round environmental campaigns that include documentaries and public-service announcements. One documentary, "Troubled Waters," which was part of the "Save Our Sounds" campaign about pollution in North Carolina's rivers, was honored by RTNDA and the Society of Professional Journalists.

"We don't need to do an environmental story every day to prove we are serious about environmental coverage," says WRAL-TV news director Doug Ballin. "It's easy to do dull, unimportant stories if you are not careful. There are just so many landfills. What environmental coverage needs most is perspective and we try to give it that."

At WCVB-TV in Boston Dave Ropeik has covered the environment full time since 1989, producing stories for the daily newscasts and an occasional series. He eschews soft features and emphasizes environmental politics and such intricate subjects as global warming and rain forests, trying to relate them to his highly educated New England audience. "The trick is to think globally and act locally," he says. "This is a solid, hard news beat and not just about nature or recycling. It's complex and technical and not easy to do right. You can't expect to be on the air every night but when you're on you know you're doing something worthwhile."

Across the country, Ropeik has a near counterpart in Scott Miller at KING-TV in Seattle. Miller has been the station's full-time environmental reporter for three years and roams the Northwest, Canada, and Alaska for stories. He has no problem finding environmental stories to air three or four times a week and goes on extended special assignments another three or four times during the year. "I can easily play off the breaking news," he says, "with a sidebar on an environmental angle. Maybe it will be about medical wastes or some court ruling on pesticides or the environmental ramifications of a fire. I don't really get into the global area but national parks, wildlife, land management on public land, fishing, toxic wastes, water, and air pollution are all part of my beat."

KGO-TV in San Francisco, WBZ-TV in Boston, KTRK-TV in Houston, and WBRZ-TV in Baton Rouge are among several stations that use their weather forecasters on environmental stories. KGO-TV, for example, converted its department into a seven-person unit it calls "The Naturalists." Its meteorologists do daily environmental reports around the weather segment, sometimes going live from the Bay Area's picturesque locations. The reports downplay the scientific aspects of the environment but cover the ecological gamut with tips and information for "everyday people."

WBZ-TV and others also use their medical and science reporters to cover the environment. Another Boston station, WLVI-TV, the UHF independent owned by Gannett, covers the environment primarily as breaking news on its 10 p.m. news but has a five-person staff that produces a half-hour environmental program every Sunday night called "Greenwatch."

Some stations entrust general-assignment reporters to include environmental stories as part of their routine. Anne Marie Bucholtz does an "Earth Watch" segment once a week for the late news at WMBD-TV in Peoria, Ill., but also covers breaking stories related to the environment.

"There are many more good stories here than you might believe," says Bucholtz, a finance major with a Master's degree in journalism who has been working in TV news for about a year. "The environment is really a great area to get into. I could probably do more if I had the time but there are other stories I have to cover as part of the general-assignment pool."

Full-time environmental reporters like WCVB-TV's Ropeik and KING-TV's Miller are few. Brad Bell at WJLA-TV in Washington is another. Bell is a former general-assignment and political reporter who was shifted full time to the environment by his news director while working at Baltimore's WMAR-TV. When the news director,

Gary Wordlaw, moved to WJLA-TV in late 1990 he recruited Bell to be the station's environmental reporter.

Bell's 90-second reports, which usually have a hard edge, are aired every Monday, Wednesday, and Friday during the second block of the 5:30 p.m. half-hour newscast. Wordlaw expects Bell's segment to help establish WJLA-TV as the "environmental station" in the market.

Nationwide, WJLA-TV is one of two network affiliates in recent years to win a Peabody—broadcasting's highest award—for its environmental coverage. In 1988 WJLA's investigative reporter Roberta Baskin was honored for her two-month radon alert campaign. And in 1989 KCNC-TV in Denver received a Peabody for a retrospective look at the Yellowstone National Park fires.

It would be gratifying—though unrealistic—if all these examples of environmental coverage on local television were indicative of an altruistic journalistic commitment. In TV news, unfortunately, one must always consider the ratings. That usually sounds crass to outsiders, particularly print critics, who somehow cannot equate newspaper and magazine circulation with television ratings. But without ratings to attract advertising dollars a newscast will founder and all the competent journalism in the world will not save it.

What's worrisome is whether this new trend toward environmental news is too much of a ratings ploy, more sensationalism than science. However, it is not necessary to sacrifice journalism for ratings. In fact, environmental reporting of the highest journalistic quality should have the best chance of attracting viewers—and raising ratings.

Radio's Environmental Journalists

In 1991, a Scripps-Howard national award for public service went to reporter/producer Art Athens of all-news WCBS-Radio in New York for a 10-part series on indoor air pollution.

That Athens and WCBS won an award is not unusual. WCBS has one of the best radio news staffs in the country.

What was unusual: The award was presented for an environmental series. For at WCBS and the approximately 11,500 other AM and FM radio stations in the United States, covering the environment is nothing special. It's just another area, albeit an important one, to be probed for news—if a station does news at all.

"We had a full-time environmental reporter for about two years, until early 1988," says Bill Yeager, the news director at all-news KFWB in Los Angeles until August 1991. "But our priorities changed. We don't ignore the environment. We cover it as breaking news. But a lot of that is the environment as it relates to transportation, car pollution, and commuter lines—part of everyday coverage in L.A."

"When you think of the environment," says Chuck Wolfe, who covers radio news for RTNDA's monthly magazine, *Communicator*, "you think of spot news. I'm not aware of any news or news-talk station that has an environmental beat reporter."

Wolfe is news director at KIKK-Radio in Houston. Bud Ward of the Environmental Health Center says Wolfe is as knowledgeable about the environment as anyone he knows in radio.

Ward also mentions Tom Meersman but Meersman does not work in commercial radio. He covers the environment, energy, and natural resources for Minnesota Public Radio in St. Paul and is one of 14 officers of the new Society of Environmental Journalists (SEJ).

There are now about 500 members of SEJ. John Nielson of National Public Radio in Washington and Charles Quimbach of Wisconsin Public Radio also belong. Along with Meersman, they were the only radio reporters listed as active members in SEJ's membership roster compiled in the spring of 1991.

"In-depth coverage of the environment," says David Bartlett, president of RTNDA, "like in-depth coverage of many complex issues, is found less and less frequently in the more narrowly targeted radio formats of the '90s."

Unless it is a breaking news story or an occasional series like the one Athens did for WCBS, the environment gets less attention in commercial radio news than it does in television news. The environment is often a subject of radio talk shows, of course, but that rarely qualifies as serious reporting or analysis. As spot news, however, the environment can sometimes be an everyday item in local radio, especially in cities with heavy concentrations of industry.

That is why Chuck Wolfe is so informed about environmental issues. The Houston area is heavily concentrated with chemical and oil facilities. "In (suburban) Deer Park," Wolfe says, "we probably have more chemical plants per square inch than anyplace in the world. Down here we have explosions and chemical fires with the release of toxic fumes on a regular basis."

Wolfe may exemplify the typical radio news director in an environmental hot spot. But he also may be typical of a journalist who tries to do the best for his profession and his medium only to be criticized by some environmental activists with a different agenda.

As most journalists know, covering an industrial accident can pose personal hazards resulting in serious illness and injury or even death. It becomes even more precarious when company officials refuse to cooperate with the media or intentionally attempt to obfuscate the situation.

Wolfe is proud of a year-long project he spearheaded that established voluntary guidelines on how to handle information on chemical hazards in the Houston area. Known as the Media Information Project, the endeavor brought together radio and television representatives, chemical plant officials, and law enforcement authorities.

"Every plant in the Houston area was involved," says Wolfe, "and the result was a 75-page report. We now have procedures that help all of us and especially the public. This is something that could be adopted nationwide."

But Wolfe's involvement cost him credibility with certain activists. "The activists see Chuck as being in bed with the chemical companies," says Bud Ward. "Nonsense," Wolfe replies. "That shows the extremes to which some of these environmental groups go when you don't follow their party line."

Considerably fewer people listen to radio than watch television for news, and radio journalists accept this fact. Although it disturbs them, it does not prevent them from doing their job, like Chuck Wolfe and Art Athens, gathering the news and presenting it to the public.

Radio is more fragmented, more selective, and more personal than other media. In covering the environment, radio news may be adequate but just barely. Thus, there would seem to be a great opportunity for radio journalists to do more environmental reporting. Like their television colleagues, however, radio reporters must learn more about the quirks of environmental journalism and become more familiar with environmental politics and terminology.

Whether they cover a chemical explosion or develop a 10-part series on pollution or simply read a wire-service report about a nuclear accident, most radio journalists could be far better prepared to cover environmental issues—even if they never have the opportunity to become full-time environmental reporters.

TV's Muddled Environmental Commitment

In the summer of 1989, Kim Standish of the newsletter *The Rundown* commissioned a survey by Frank N. Magid Associates to determine the issues that were of most interest to the television audience. Environment topped the poll, cited by 80 percent of the survey's respondents.

To some news directors and their consultants, the *Rundown* survey only confirmed what they had been discovering in their own research and during ascertainment sessions with community leaders. Environment was hot.

Magid and other TV news consultants like Audience Research & Development (ARD) and McHugh & Hoffman, advised their clients to implement or to enhance their environmental coverage.

ARD, in particular, made an elaborate environmental presentation to its clients at the RTNDA convention in Kansas City in September 1989. ARD offered clients a "turnkey" outline with several recommendations to get stations quickly into environmental reporting. Create an "E-Team," ARD said. "1. *Franchise it!* Designate an environmental specialist to spearhead your coverage. Develop a special title and graphic for this segment."

By Earth Day 1990, environmental stories were saturating local newscasts around the country. The quality varied but the quantity was there. The environment was red hot!

A year later the ardor had cooled. "The environment is still important but not like it was prior to the Earth Day push in 1990," admits

Jim Willi, executive vice president at ARD. "We still see it in our research but it's no longer as intense."

Other consultants concur. "We've seen environmental interest fall to fourth in our 1991 surveys," says Eric Braun, vice president of consulting for Magid. "The environment now tends to be geographically specific like in Oregon, Maine, Northern California, and Washington."

"News directors allocated resources to cover everything leading up to Earth Day but now those resources are going elsewhere," says Mackie Morris, another Magid consultant. "And with the second and third wave of newsroom cutbacks, environmental reporting is part of the mix, fighting for air time with crime, the economy, and everything else. The (Persian Gulf) War diverted everyone's attention so whether this (reduction of environmental coverage) is permanent or just a down cycle is the question."

"The environment is no less important," says Roy Meyer, executive vice president of McHugh & Hoffman. "Our studies clearly show that viewers want more of it, but more thorough and thoughtful stuff. If they don't get it, they will go somewhere else. The real dilemma is that there is just so much staff and resources at each station and it's an individual choice on which subject gets priority."

The environment may no longer be a priority at stations with past achievements. Doug Ballin admits education and health get more emphasis at WRAL-TV in Raleigh. "The quality of our state schools and how we're going to pay for them has become a much bigger story," Ballin says. "Crime is a growing problem in an area not historically known for crime. The problem with the environment is that no burning issue exists in people's minds, unless you do something in their backyard."

John Hollenhorst emphasized environmental stories for KSL-TV in Salt Lake City until he left on a journalism fellowship sabbatical in the fall of 1990. When he returned in mid-1991, the station's environmental commitment had diminished and Hollenhorst was assigned to a more general news beat.

WFAA-TV in Dallas is one of the premier news stations in the country, having won every major award in TV news over the last 20 years.

But it has never had a full-time environmental specialist despite executive news director Marty Haag's passion for the environment.

"Two years ago I pitched going down to the Amazon to do something on the rain forest," he says. "But we decided it would take too much time and too much money.

"Now, maybe you can criticize me on that. But, at the same time, I had someone working full time on the S&L story and that person, Byron Harris, is credited with breaking that one. The environment is increasingly important to us but there just aren't enough bodies to assign someone full time. It's that simple."

Eric Braun says viewers seem to crave environmental news primarily when they are personally involved. "No one cares about owls and snail darters," he says. "They want to know about the 'air I can't breathe' or 'the water I can't drink.'"

Jim Snyder, the long-time Post-Newsweek Stations vice president, pinpoints the dilemma for news directors trying to balance journalism with the need for ratings.

"Environmental reporting just isn't the element that will turn markets around or be the tie-breaker," he says. "But it *is* important and local news directors need to do more than just turn to environmental reporting when there is a major story. It may be too late by then."

Roy Meyer believes outsiders should not be overly critical of stations that have de-emphasized environmental reporting. "Everyone has had to adjust to the economic realities of today," he says. "Remember, it (environmental reporting) was virtually non-existent three years ago and today there are environmental units of some type in most local stations in the major markets. That's a pretty good track record. What stations have to guard against is being too trendy. That's where their credibility will suffer."

In general, the news media—print and electronic—are traditionally trendy. Pack journalism is more the rule than the exception. The media get overly excited about particular subjects while casually ignoring others, flitting from one hot topic to another. That occurs even more in local TV news which is notorious for being an unabashed copycat.

The journalistic peril is that serious and complex issues sometimes get mangled in the process. Environmental coverage is a perfect example.

Now, there's nothing wrong with covering stories about disposable diapers, recycling, and fast-food containers. They're all part of the environmental story. But it is more difficult and time consuming to start explaining how global warming and the Brazilian rain forests relate to the survival of the local community.

Of course, any coverage of the environment (no matter how superficial), if honest and truthful, is better than none. But in using traditional TV news methods to determine environmental coverage and priorities, local TV newscasts may be performing a minor service on one hand while grossly misleading the public on the other.

That's why it is essential that even general-assignment reporters who occasionally cover environmental stories receive some basic training about environmental journalism. Assignment editors and producers who supervise the reporters should too, for it is their decisions that usually determine what the public sees in any specific newscast. Above all, the news director must be knowledgeable for he or she must ensure the integrity of that coverage even as it is utilized in the overall strategy to gain ratings.

And that's where the problem of marketing and hype comes in. "Establishing a franchise" has become a familiar element in local TV news. The "franchise" can be in any area: sports, consumer, health, etc. It becomes part of the marketing and promotion that not only attracts viewers but helps form the station's long-term news image.

If a franchise such as an "E-Team" or "Doctor Earth" or "The Naturalists" can provide substantive and enlightening information on the environment, so be it. But there is a danger that content may be overshadowed by merchandising.

Surely, everyone realizes that a highly promoted series on pesticides or radon that doesn't live up to the viewer's expectations is self-destructive. But so is the embellishment of a franchise—"The Green Team" for example—which delivers superficiality instead of substance.

There's also a concern that environmental reporting will be defiled by the sales department. At some stations environmental segments are offered to advertisers for special sponsorships within a newscast. Segment sponsorship is an old and highly questionable practice that has regained popularity in the wake of diminishing revenue sources.

"I see nothing wrong with sponsorships as long as the sponsor has no control over the editorial content," says WJLA-TV's Gary Wordlaw in defending the sponsorship of Brad Bell's 90-second reports. "Our station management weighs very carefully every potential sponsor to avoid compromising our journalistic integrity."

But Bell admits he is uneasy about being sponsored. "You can lose credibility quickly if you do a series on pesticides and lawn care and it's sponsored by a weed killer," he says. "There is a terrible dark side when the sales department is involved. I think this is the biggest risk to environmental reporting right now."

III. Risk Assessment and Science of the Environment

Any radio or TV journalist involved in coverage of environmental stories must comprehend the meaning of the words "risk assessment," "risk management," "risk perception," and "risk communication." They are terms that are crucial to the environmental public-policy debate.

It is imperative that reporters, news directors, and producers fully understand the implications of these essential environmental "risk" words. That's because journalists have the critical responsibility of explaining it all to the listener and viewer.

The resolution of environmental dilemmas based on risk assessment, risk management, risk perception, and risk communication depends on a consensus among politicians, bureaucrats, scientists, environmentalists, the media—and, most significantly—the public. Ultimately it is the public, through its influence on the politicians and bureaucrats, that determines EPA policy and, thus, the priorities for solving environmental problems.

The resolution of environmental problems almost always requires tradeoffs between money and health. This is one of the more controversial aspects of environmental risks. There is just so much money available to resolve so many environmental problems—be they local or global. Some activists want finite solutions, or "zero-risk." A more rational approach considers the "acceptable risk."

These opposing theories are simple to understand. Zero-risk means spending as much money as necessary on an environmental problem to eliminate all risks to any individual. But if 98 percent of the risks are eradicated, is it necessary to eliminate the last 2 percent if the risks are minimal and the costs to do so are astronomical? Thus, an acceptable risk is determined through a cost-benefit analysis.

Despite the devout belief of some zero-risk activists, most environmentalists and government officials believe economic costs make it impossible to solve every environmental problem without some compromises. "There simply are more anxieties than we can possibly create laws to alleviate, and far more risks than resources to eliminate them," writes William K. Reilly, administrator of the EPA. "Nothing is 100-percent safe. Neither are all the risks equal."[14]

In its most simple and severe terms, this environmental tradeoff philosophy can be compared to the classic survival story of a lifeboat taking on water more quickly than its occupants can remove it. Eventually, some passengers will have to go overboard—voluntarily or by force—for others to stay alive. The ultimate outcome of this lamentable dilemma comes down to choices—by the group or by individuals; choices that are often callous and political and dependent on myriad social and economic factors.

But to truly compare this lifeboat illustration to the environmental risk dilemma another element must be added. What if the lifeboat were drifting in fog so thick that the passengers could not see each other? Nor could they determine with certainty how badly the boat was leaking or how close they were to land. Information on any of those factors could help improve the odds of survival for all. But, there's a splash and a passenger is gone and none of the survivors knows who it is or why he or she left.

The fog is comparable to the contradictory scientific evidence that surrounds many of our environmental debates. Scientists frequently disagree on the seriousness of a particular environmental problem and the ways to solve it. Like the fog enshrouding the lifeboat, the scientific contradiction is the fateful element that can distort the seriousness of an environmental dilemma and its eventual harm.

Thus, in the final analysis of environmental risks, a decision based on contradictory scientific findings and limited funds ultimately may have to be made about whether the health and welfare of some should be sacrificed, if necessary, to save the lives of many. But, of course, the issue is not always so terminal. And the choices are much more complex.

Several books and dozens of newspaper and magazine articles have addressed the subject of risk in varying detail and it has become, increasingly, a major topic for panel discussions at environmental seminars for journalists. Radio and television journalists covering the environment would be negligent if they did not learn more about risk assessment, risk management, risk perception, and risk communication. The following section offers a brief introduction. The selected bibliography at the end of this publication can serve as a recommended reading list.

Definition of Risks

Risk is a seminal word in the environmental vocabulary. It is a measure of the possibility, probability, or chance of incurring loss or injury because of factors that could be dangerous or hazardous.

Thus, there is a risk of developing cancer and dying because of exposure to smoking cigarettes. The probability of that occurring depends, in part, on how much smoking an individual does over a specific period of time.

Each risk has a value that is measured against other risks. So, one can gauge the risk value of smoking cigarettes against that of smoking cigars; or the risk value of living near a toxic dump site to living near a nuclear power plant; or the risk value of smoking cigarettes to that of living near a nuclear power plant.

From this definition of risk come its environmental progeny—risk assessment, risk management, risk perception, and risk communication.

Risk communication is probably the easiest term to understand. It has been defined succinctly as "any communication that informs people about the existence, nature, form, severity, or acceptability of risks."[15] Risk communication is, characteristically, a negative process since it deals fundamentally with hazards and dangers. Corporations, in particular, have made risk communication an integral part of their public relations endeavors. It is the standard lexicon in coping with environmental emergencies and in promoting environmental products.

Perhaps the most successful and experienced practitioner of environmental risk communication is Hill and Knowlton Inc., the international public relations firm, which frequently is hired by corporations during an environmental or health crisis. The agency has been involved with many of the major environmental stories of the last two decades, from Three Mile Island to the Alar controversy. Hill and Knowlton has been so effective in molding and changing public perceptions in the aftermath of crises that some activists are as critical of Hill and Knowlton as they are of the corporations it represents.

Risk assessment is the most critical term for determining the risk value of any environmental or health concern. It is frequently misused by the public and the media who confuse it with risk management.

Risk assessment is a technical term that pertains strictly to the scientific analysis of risk. The term refers to the analytical techniques used to estimate risks and identify hazards, but excludes other factors— such as emotional, social, political, and cost considerations—that could color the scientific findings. When these components are integrated into the evaluation of the risk, it becomes risk management.

Through risk management, then, the economic costs and benefits associated with the risk are evaluated to determine public policy toward eliminating, reducing, or minimizing the risk. Risk management weighs the alternatives and tradeoffs in an attempt to establish a minimum risk level, below which a risk can reasonably be ignored.

Whenever risk management is attempted, one must measure the short term against the long term in an equation that involves the risk and the benefit. Money is the wild card.

To one degree or another, every environmental issue has a risk value. Some are more precarious than others. Some are more foreboding. Some are more emotional. And some are more parochial and framed by special interests.

A fundamental question asked in risk management is: How much money should be spent over what period of time to achieve what benefit? In answering, short-term benefits frequently are measured against the long-term and the costs of each solution are weighed against each other. Often, the tradeoffs are ambiguous.

Consider, for example, the debates over the use of plastic versus paper cups by fast-food franchisers, and disposable versus cloth diapers. There is no clear evidence that one is more detrimental to the environment than the other. But there is a cost factor involving energy use, recycling, and landfills. Choosing biodegradable plastic over paper and cloth diapers over disposables may produce a lower (or higher) cost that may not correlate with any long-term benefits that are better or worse for the environment.

"The problem with risk management is that there is no widespread agreement on the values," says Ford Rowan, a former NBC reporter who is now an attorney specializing in the environment. "In a democracy, the values of scientists, activists, politicians, or reporters are no better or worse than anybody else's. Who is to say how much should be spent to reduce how much risk and to save how many lives over what time span?"

Risk assessment has become a cornerstone of EPA policy for resolving many environmental problems. But it is controversial, in part, because risk assessment is mandated in some federal laws and regulations as a major determining element of policy—meaning the rational cost-benefit evaluation inherent in risk management is negated.

"The Superfund legislation galvanized the risk assessment movement," says Bud Ward. "The EPA was turned into an anti-cancer agency as a deliberate political decision by the Carter Administration. But as we clean up hazardous waste sites, we are finding that some are not worth it because the risks are low and the costs are high. Yet, decisions continue to be made solely on risk assessment.

"And, this risk assessment interpretation has been upheld by the courts and reaffirmed by Congress. A major part of the decisions on clean air standards were reached without regard to the technological feasibility or costs. Of course, this isn't true with all the laws. Under the pesticide law, EPA was specifically required to consider the economic tradeoffs and cost-benefits of some pesticides. One can only speculate, and hope, that in the privacy of the twelfth-floor conference room, the EPA considers costs and technology in its risk assessment. Otherwise, it would bankrupt the country," says Ward.

Harvey M. Sapolsky, professor of public policy and organization at the Massachusetts Institute of Technology, believes government policies add to the confusion over risk.

"Convinced that they must appear willing to alleviate every product or environmental fear as it arises," he writes, "officials make no effort to pursue consistent, carefully designed policies toward health risks. Whatever the scare of the day, officials stand ready to formulate quickly congressional testimony, briefing papers, news releases, and programs that demonstrate their unsurpassed commitment to protecting the public. Dare they hesitate, and an ambitious congressman armed with staff and a subcommittee will leap forward to take their place in front of the cameras."[16]

To appreciate the quandary of the EPA, however, a reporter must be cognizant of the outside pressures and criticism from "both ends of the environmental political spectrum," as Professor Vincent Covello of Columbia University has written.

"Proponents of less restrictive environmental regulation have charged that techniques and assumptions used in EPA risk assessments reflect unjustified bias in favor of overly protective risk management values," writes Covello, who directs Columbia's Center for Risk Communication. "Environmentalists, on the other hand, have argued precisely the opposite, claiming that risk assessments used to support EPA decisions reflect techniques and assumptions that understate risks for the purpose of relieving regulatory burdens on industrial polluters."[17]

Even when risk assessment and risk management are employed equitably in forging environmental public policy, there is another component that complicates the denouement: the public's perception of risk.

What the public perceives as a risk may depend less on factual information than on emotions, attitudes, and opinions. For instance, activities over which an individual has control (such as cigarette smoking and automobile driving) are likely to be perceived as less risky than activities beyond the individual's control (like flying as an airplane passenger).

Nowadays, public perceptions of environmental risks generally differ from scientific reality, and sometimes quite sharply. For example, the public believes toxins from hazardous waste sites, radiation from nuclear power plants, and pollution from oil spills are major environmental risks, even though scientific experts rank all three as relatively low risks. Correspondingly, the experts rate global warming and the destruction of natural habitats through soil erosion and deforestation as the highest environmental risks but the public perceives these as low risks.

This disparity between the experts' assessment of risk and the public's perception startled the EPA and its Science Advisory Board after officials reviewed the results of a Roper poll commissioned by the advisory board in late 1990. What worries the EPA is the effect these distorted public perceptions may have on Congress in passing environmental legislation and setting priorities.

In January 1991, the EPA told a Senate hearing chaired by Daniel Patrick Moynihan (D-N.Y.) that scientists' views—risk assessment—must take precedence over public perceptions. EPA Administrator William K. Reilly testified that the United States cannot afford to spend money for environmental protection "in the wrong places."

"If there is a source of trustworthy information that can lend authority and coherence in helping characterize and even rank risk, it is good science," Reilly wrote in a *Washington Post* op-ed piece later that year. "In my opinion, the environmental debate has long suffered from too little science. There has been plenty of emotion and politics, but scientific data have not always been featured prominently in environmental efforts, and have sometimes been ignored even when available."[18]

The EPA approach has the fervent support of President Bush whose 1992 budget includes a 10-page tract that encourages the revamping of government priorities on the environment and other areas based on scientific judgments.

But some senators—and many others concerned with the environment—are wary of depending exclusively on scientific information to set priorities. They reason that science is "imprecise" and even among respected scientists there are disagreements, often monumental ones. Then there are the biases, self-interests, and political beliefs of the scientists themselves, some of whom may have especially acute biases on specific environmental issues.

"All science, not just environmental science, is almost always uncertain, or uncertain to a degree," writes Victor Cohn, the veteran *Washington Post* science specialist.[19] "Even the most honest and most eminent scientists disagree when the results of their studies are in conflict, or evidence is incomplete."[20]

Citing a 1984 Twentieth Century Fund task force report, Cohn adds that "the main offenders on all sides are scientists for government, industry, and environmental groups who 'make sweeping judgments on the basis of incomplete and hence inadequate data,' stress their own opinions, and omit or minimize conflicting evidence."[21]

Even if the scientific information is valid, the public's perception of a risk usually is framed by the media and special-interest groups. And it is here that the environmental battles over public policies are usually won and lost.

That all sides try to manipulate the media is a given. Even the fairest and most objective journalist can be exploited. But that's because the very nature of journalism enables anyone with a cause or an opinion to be heard.

As some critics of environmental coverage have stated, journalism is often reactive in approach, impatient in practice, and fascinated by conflict, aberration, and controversy. Reporters and editors have little affinity for the technical and complex, particularly in television where simplicity is encouraged because of the viewer's short attention span. Thus, there is a tendency to oversimplify and to find easy answers to complex issues. Often these answers do not reflect reality but result from the clash of scientific information.

In absorbing what the media report about scientific information, it is little wonder that the public often comes away with distorted perceptions of risk. MIT's Sapolsky writes:

> Consumers must rely upon the risk interpretations of intermediaries—scientists, government officials, reporters, policy advocates, and others—to guide their behavior. The intermediaries often provide misleading advice. Their views on risks are shaped by professional and organizational interests that encourage, in most instances, the exaggeration of dangers. Their presentation of risks makes small risks become big and big risks bigger, but not proportionally. Consumers are easily confused, thinking health risks are bigger and more alike than they actually are....

> It is not that consumers are intentionally misled. On the contrary, much of the distortion is the unavoidable consequence of professions and organizations competing with one another for scarce resources, in this instance the patronage of a population frightened by the recognition of its own mortality. Scientists, individually and by disciplines, compete for recognition and reward; reporters must seek out audiences; public-interest advocates need patronage; and government officials have to obtain budgets for their agencies. Even product manufacturers, who might be thought always to wish to underplay risks, can find market advantage in stimulating fears by heralding product versions free of suspect ingredients. Proportionality is easily lost in the clamor for attention and support.[22]

Often, the result of all this is costly public policy with narrow or limited benefits.

Attorney Rowan sums it up best:

> In theory, our choices in solving environmental problems are supposed to start with risk assessment and be evaluated in a risk management model. But, in reality, public risk perceptions drive the public-policy process. When interest groups and activists get involved, we usually end up with policymaking by the decibel level.

Of course, the decibel level might be lowered considerably by better reporting from journalists—especially on television.

Scientific Sources

Covering the scientific aspects of environmental and health issues can be a quagmire even for experienced journalists. For a general-assignment TV reporter thrust occasionally into an environmental crisis, the science can be overwhelming.

Journalists are rightfully criticized for their lack of comprehension and ignorance on scientific matters. But some of the criticism is absurd. Certainly, reporters need to learn as much as they can about subjects they are covering. However, it is impossible for all reporters and their supervising producers or editors to be as knowledgeable about science as some critics demand.

Critics have a legitimate point, though, in challenging the culture and standards of the journalistic profession. Clearly, in the competitive media menagerie, there is a tendency to oversimplify, dramatize, and polarize issues. When dealing with technical matters, inaccurate interpretation often results. Thus, scientists not only distrust the media but blame them for unnecessarily causing public fear and anxiety.

"The news media are bored by institutional and systemic problems and show little interest in incremental change," writes Stephen Klaidman, a senior fellow at Georgetown University's Kennedy Institute of Ethics. "Until there is a crisis, the media rarely report persistently and in-depth on subjects like regulation of the savings and loan industry....Unless a development in science or medicine can be presented as a breakthrough, if only a mini-breakthrough, it will usually get scant coverage. When it does make it as news, conclusions are often inflated, either by researchers in press conferences and interviews or by reporters."[23]

Klaidman and others are particularly critical of the criteria journalists use in choosing scientific sources. This criticism focuses on three specific areas: (1) The range of sources is too narrow and limited; (2) reporters are not skeptical enough and thus sources are not challenged; and (3) there is too much effort to reach a journalistic "balance."

But even the critics cannot agree on the guidelines.

Narrow Choice of Sources

If there is a consensus among critics, it is that far too often government officials are the prime source of information in environmental stories. Some critics charge that corporate sources are overly used. Still others feel the media listen too much to environmental activists. But, mostly it is government officials who are faulted.

The 1989 survey by the Center for Media and Public Affairs cited in Chapter 1 documented the dependence on government as a source in environmental stories. The Bush Administration, Congress, and other government officials accounted for 32 percent of the sources used by the networks and weekly news magazines, twice the amount of any other group.

Sharon Friedman of Lehigh University has studied scientific sources for almost a decade. She notes that "there are a number of reasons for a dependence" on the government.

"Government officials are considered credible and authoritative," she writes. "They often are easy to reach, and many are used to talking to reporters. Journalists rightly point out that they need to talk to government sources as they are the ones either administering the laws or regulating environmental hazards. However, using government officials as sources too often leaves a reporter open for manipulation."[24]

That was freely admitted in a 1988 *Columbia Journalism Review* article by a former EPA press officer, Jim Sibbison. Sibbison, who was pushing his own anti-Reagan/Bush Administration agenda, chastised Washington reporters for relying too heavily on EPA press releases.

"I helped to prepare the releases and carefully monitored a lot of EPA stories in those days," Sibbison wrote. "A host of reporters produced a lot of EPA stories in those days. But all they had to do was rewrite our material and possibly call an environmental group for comment. It was a textbook case of spoonfeeding."[25]

Even when reporters go beyond the press releases, they consistently turn to government scientists. "Journalists depend on scientists affiliated with major government and private research centers because newsworthy developments are likely to come from their labs," says Klaidman. "Journalists also depend on scientists who can express themselves clearly and provocatively in laymen's language because, to put the best gloss on it, these researchers explain science clearly for non-scientists, or at worst, in sound bites."[26]

Friedman says the problem is even more acute for general-assignment reporters. "Often they do not have the time to cultivate sources, even local ones, who can help them interpret technical information," she writes. "(Many have) little idea of the multitude of national environmental and scientific organizations they could call on for assistance."[27]

Challenging Sources

Because of the complex and technical nature of what they are reporting, journalists usually are reluctant to challenge their sources of information. This is one area where the critics agree.

"Environmental issues are too important for journalists not to live up to their pesky skepticism," writes former reporter John Maxwell Hamilton of the World Bank. "They have to ask 'so what' questions even when doing so seems rank heresy."[28]

Cornell science professor Dorothy Nelkin says journalists are too much in awe of scientists. "Journalists, particularly those with limited experience in science reporting, are vulnerable to manipulation by their sources of information—who are, in most cases, scientists," she writes.[29]

"Reporters faced with deadlines are too often ready to accept the ideology that science is a neutral source of authority, an objective judge of truth. Many journalists (even those who have little formal training in science or the scientific method) frequently adopt the mindset or 'frame' of scientists; they interpret science in terms defined by their sources, even when those sources are clearly interested in projecting a particular view."[30]

Victor Cohn warns of bad science hidden behind special interests. "A few (scientists)...can be dishonest," he writes. "Many more are subject to biases, prejudices, economic interests, and political leanings that can color judgment."[31]

That reality has been emphasized in recent years with several reports of dishonesty and malfeasance by scientists researching science and health subjects. One 73-page report by the House Government Operations Committee in 1990 cited 10 cases of alleged misconduct at several universities and the National Institutes of Health.

"We reporters tend to rely most on 'authorities' who are either most colorfully quotable or quickly quotable, and these authorities often tend to be those who get most carried away or who have the biggest axes to grind," writes Cohn. "Without being cynical and believing nothing—an automatic disqualification for any journalist—a reporter should be equally skeptical and greet every claim by saying 'show me.'"[32]

Balanced Sources

Striving for balance is fundamental to traditional journalism. And where environmental science is concerned, journalists are snared in the middle of the debate on just what "balance" means.

Some critics believe the effort to achieve balance in science issues frequently gives too much credibility to fringe elements. "If 90 percent of the scientific thought is on one side, the media will give equal time to the other 10 percent and call that balance," notes Ford Rowan.

In a comprehensive manual for sources developed by a group of Rutgers professors, *Risk Communication for Environmental News Sources*, the authors write:

"[The] balanced treatment conveys...the notion that one side is as credible as the other....But often one side represents mainstream scientific thought, while the other is a minority dissident voice....The scientific establishment, like any establishment, sometimes turns out systematically wrong, [but] the scientific majority usually turns out closer to the mark than the mavericks. It is deceptive to present such opposing positions as if they had equal support."[33]

But other critics believe the minority scientific view is often just part of the process toward achieving the truth since science is imperfect.

"Even when responsible opinion on an issue is clustered in the center," writes Stephen Klaidman, "an otherwise unassailable journalistic account will sometimes provide 'balance' by juxtaposing the comments of quotable 'experts' whose views seem relatively extreme....The sources chosen for their polar views are more often than not respectable members of the scientific establishment whose opinions on unsettled questions differ sharply only because one takes the most conservative position that can be sustained by the data, and the other, the most radical."[34]

To put both views on balance in perspective, one can think of no better example than the Alar controversy. There, a minority scientific opinion about an apple pesticide was given more than equal treatment by the media despite compelling contradictory evidence from the so-called center of scientific thought.

Credible Sources

Even the most diligent reporters, however, probably will be criticized because of the sources they use. It may be simply the consequence of one's point of view.

As Cornell's Nelkin sums up the dilemma: "Industry groups and some scientists accuse reporters of taking a biased, sensational, anti-technology approach to reporting risks; they blame the press for creating unwarranted fear of technology. Meanwhile, other scientists, mainly environmentalists as well as consumer advocates, accuse the press of relying unfairly and almost exclusively on 'establishment' expertise and of burying stories that might challenge local industries."[35]

If journalists are to avoid or at least reduce criticism of their environmental coverage, they must do a better job of interpreting scientific sources, and not just selecting them. In their writings, such aforementioned observers as Klaidman, Cohn, Nelkin, Friedman, and others offer various suggestions on how to best accomplish this. Their books and articles are referenced at the end of this publication and readers are urged to consult them for a more detailed explanation of the subject. Cohn's books are particularly noteworthy for their simplicity in synthesizing scientific information from a reporter's perspective.

Several points on sources need to be stressed to journalists:

—First and foremost, be skeptical but not cynical about what you are told. There is a significant difference—cynicism is a negative that will slow the truth-seeking process.

—As a skeptic, practice the golden rules of ABC's Roger Caras who says: "Avoid like a plague anyone who seems reluctant or unable to say 'I don't know.' Avoid people who say 'forever' and 'never' for that is an extremely long time. Avoid people who make predictions arbitrarily beyond 25 years for that's not reality, that's science fiction. And avoid people who know all the answers because they are the types who make it all up."

—Be wary of statistics no matter who produces and reports them. Research can be deceptive depending on sundry elements, and statistics can be made to prove whatever the researcher wants them to. Even statistics and research reviewed by peers and published in prestigious magazines and journals should not be accepted without challenge.

—Be careful when comparing one set of statistics to another for it may be a subtle but significant argument comparing apples to oranges. And make every attempt to give the statistics perspective and context to prevent the numbers from becoming a blur.

—Don't be afraid to ask dumb questions. If reporters do not thoroughly understand what they are being told, how can they explain it intelligently to listeners and viewers?

—Identify the politics, special interests, and funding of groups, public relations firms, and individuals making claims. That may say more about the truth of their scientific boasts than anything else.

—Don't immediately assume one side is right because it is identified as an "environmentalist" and the other side wrong because it is a corporation (or vice versa). That's presumptuous at best, and prejudicial and arrogant at worst.

"It's hard not to pick sides without experience," says Rae Tyson of *USA Today*. "It's difficult dealing with corporations that have no personalities and with companies or businesses that may have done damage and have something to hide. It's much easier to develop allies on the other side but they are often wearing black hats that you don't see."

—Finally, do not get emotionally involved with the subject or the environmental cause being advocated.

"I've found reporters so guided by emotion that they tend to bounce right by scientific facts," says Bill Winters, the long-time New York director of public affairs for General Motors Corporation.

"Too many environmental reporters think of themselves as the stewards of 'Mother Earth,'" says Dave Ropeik of WCVB-TV in Boston. "They forget they have a press pass."

That is not only self defeating; it is not journalism. And it is a risky betrayal of the public trust.

IV. Where Do We Go From Here?

Sharon Friedman is exasperated. After more than a decade of studying the media's coverage of environmental crises, the Lehigh University science journalism professor wonders why the media keep making the same mistakes. "You would think they would learn," she says, singling out television in particular for being unresponsive to the criticisms leveled at past environmental coverage.

Dave Ropeik is frustrated. He understands news priorities and is gratified that the management at WCVB-TV in Boston considers environmental reporting important enough to make it his full-time assignment. But he wonders why everyone in the newsroom does not find the environment as newsworthy as he does. "It takes extra convincing to let me do stories because few people in TV news have a sense of what environmental reporting is all about," he says.

In their anxieties, Friedman and Ropeik share a commonality that is irrefutable. Electronic journalists need to get a better grasp of environmental journalism and all its ramifications. They don't need to be experts on the environment—but they do need knowledge and comprehension. Reporting on the environment must improve. The public's perceptions must be changed. Local television is not the panacea. But it is part of the problem and part of the solution.

It shouldn't take an environmental crisis like a nuclear accident or an oil spill to show how reporting can be improved. It can be accomplished every day on those 6- and 11-o'clock newscasts.

"I'm not asking to be treated any differently in getting air time than the person who covers politics or crime," says Ropeik. "I just think the gatekeepers need to adjust their news values. They need to get away from the stereotypes and cliches about environmental reporting, thinking it's only about recycling or nature or some soft feature, and realize it is hard news. If editors and producers don't take it seriously as hard news, how can the public?"

Assigning someone like Ropeik to cover the environment full time may not be economically feasible in many newsrooms. A health-and-medical reporter can do environmental stories. So can meteorologists and weather forecasters and weekend anchors as long as they understand the issues and treat them seriously. But economics shouldn't be an excuse for inept or incomplete coverage.

With just a little time, effort, and commitment anyone in the newsroom can learn more about how to cover the environment. Plenty of resources are available, ranging from on-line computer services no more than a phone call away to extensive seminars and courses on university campuses. These can be especially helpful to general-assignment reporters, assignment editors, and producers who must be knowledgeable about the myriad subjects juggled into a daily newscast.

Several books referenced elsewhere in this publication should prove instructive for background purposes, and can be obtained at little or no cost from the publisher.

What one discovers in perusing these books is the cross-referencing that makes information so easily available for anyone who seriously wants it.

There are several newsletters that monitor environmental issues and environmental journalism. One of the best is Bud Ward's monthly *Environment Writer* which covers environmental journalism's activities, problems, controversies, and ethics. It also tracks major environmental stories in both the mainstream and environmental trade press and stories aired on the networks. The quarterly publication of the new Society of Environmental Journalists, *SEJournal*, is similar to Ward's newsletter but provides different perspectives and longer articles written by practicing environmental journalists.

Two computer-based resources are the Meeman Archive at the University of Michigan and the new *Greenwire* in Falls Church, Va. Meeman provides articles on conservation, natural resources, and the environment, while *Greenwire* offers subscribers a daily compendium of environmental issues, including developments in Congress and the EPA, and a synopsis of stories appearing in newspapers, magazines, and on network television.

The Science Journalism Center at the University of Missouri offers *Inquiry*, a newsletter for science writers, and also provides background material on environmental issues through its newspaper and magazine clipping service. The Scientists Institute for Public Information in New York is another organization that assists reporters in researching issues and provides spokespersons and videotape background material including stock footage and video news releases for the electronic media.

Both organizations are among several that also sponsor seminars and forums periodically for environmental journalists. Others include the sponsors of this publication—The Media Institute and the Radio and Television News Directors Foundation (through their joint program, the Environmental Reporting Forum); the Foundation for American Communications in Los Angeles; and the Poynter Institute of St. Petersburg, Fla.

This is not an all-inclusive list of sources, of course, but only a sampling of what is available to assist environmental journalists.

One does not have to be a specialist in the environment to understand the nuances of environmental reporting. Politics. Distortions. Manipulation. Complex explanations. Scientific contradictions. Emotions. They're all part of the mix.

So is the journalistic agenda. For local television news this can be one of the biggest impediments to original, worthwhile environmental reporting. It is typical of local stations to follow a national journalistic agenda. The influence of this agenda on the daily decisions in a local newsroom cannot be underestimated. This, more than anything else, accounts for the pack mentality that so often distorts or exaggerates an environmental crisis.

The agenda is usually set by a small group of elite media organizations whose power base is in the New York-Washington corridor. The *New York Times*, *Wall Street Journal*, *Washington Post*, *USA Today*, and the ABC, NBC, and CBS networks are at the forefront. What they print and air forms the core of news for that day or week or month. Others sometimes contribute to the agenda—a story in the *Los Angeles Times*, *Miami Herald*, or *Newsweek*, or one distributed by the Associated Press or aired by CNN, for example. Frequently there is news so big it cannot be ignored. But the national media provide the background and continuity that has become the essence of daily news.

It's not that there is collusion among a handful of influential media outlets. It's simply that the journalistic practice of follow-the-leader is commonly accepted within the business. The danger, of course, is pack journalism, indolence, and the absence of independent thinking and skepticism.

A telling example of how this affects environmental reporting came during the historic high-level environmental symposium sponsored by the Smithsonian Institution in 1989. The all-day gathering brought together journalists, scientists, and politicians in what was promoted as an urgent discussion of potentially calamitous environmental problems.

Panelist after panelist warned of the dire consequences of global warming and overpopulation. It was virtually a one-sided examination of some very controversial and debatable issues. Opposing views were almost non-existent. Many of the journalists on hand endorsed advocacy journalism on behalf of the environment. Others simply acquiesced, confessing ignorance or confusion.

Leslie Stahl, then covering the White House for CBS, moderated a panel on global warming. What she said in her introduction is revealing. "As a person who does not cover this issue," she said, "my education comes from stories in the *Washington Post* and the *New*

York Times, like the one this week in the *Post* about climate studies and global warming and I get very confused." If everyone depended solely on the *Post* or *Times* or the networks for information about the environment they would be confused, too. Not that those two newspapers or CBS are wrong or right. They have been both.

Leslie Stahl is a solid journalist. But, like others in and out of Washington, she is ensnared in a journalistic syndrome that is myopic and self destructive.

Local television news needs to break away from this agenda-setting morass. It needs more independent reporters like Dave Ropeik in Boston and Scott Miller at KING-TV in Seattle, and it needs more innovative news directors, producers, and assignment editors willing to break journalistic traditions and icons.

The environment is a global problem and a local problem and the problems are intertwined. The public needs to know that. There may be toxins from a nearby plant in one's backyard today but there may be acid rain from Germany there tomorrow.

In June 1992, a major international environmental conference is scheduled for Rio de Janeiro, Brazil. Known as the Earth Summit, the two-week meeting is expected to draw more than 30,000 participants including 70 heads of state from 170 nations. The world's major ecological problems will be discussed, including global warming, protection of plants and animals, and preservation of rain forests. The United Nations, which is sponsoring the conference, believes the meeting will produce new international policies for resolving environmental problems into the next century.

Is this a local story?

Absolutely.

It may not seem like a local story, but the Earth Summit will have long-term consequences that will make coverage by local radio and television stations imperative. That doesn't mean stations need to dispatch crews to Rio. It does mean that local stations should make a commitment toward covering the Earth Summit through network and syndicated feeds direct from Brazil tied in with locally produced sidebars and analytical features about how all of this affects the hometown "backyard."

• • •

Despite the animosity and bitterness of the past, there are new signs of compromise and cooperation within the environmental arena. In mid-August of 1991, for instance, a compromise was reached among historic rivals in environmental groups and the oil industry over requirements to reformulate cleaner burning gasoline, which was part of the Clean Air Act amendments.

In reporting on the arrangement, *Washington Post* environmental specialist Michael Weisskopf wrote that "the terms of the agreement, and the way it was forged in a process known as regulatory negotiation, give the deal an importance beyond gasoline. The signatories, representing a range of traditionally warring interests—oil companies, clean-fuel manufacturers, environmental and consumer groups—are bound not to litigate or lobby against regulations that implement their compromises....By demonstrating the effectiveness of reg-neg (regulatory negotiation) in translating contentious laws into regulation, the deal is expected to increase usé of this practice across the government."[36]

Some observers believed the defeat of environmental initiatives by voters in five states in the 1990 elections was a result of a backlash against overly aggressive special-interest groups. Others argued that the public simply does not trust government to resolve environmental problems. The election-day losses may have sent a signal to the special-interest groups on both sides and to politicians that the environment *is* too important to be politicized. The new agreement on gasoline requirements may be an indication that someone is paying attention.

• • •

Researching this monograph has intensified my interest in environmental issues and in the coverage of those issues. It has become instinctive for me, now, to challenge my students in Northwestern's graduate broadcast program whenever covering environmental, health, and science stories. In particular, I have pointedly advised my students to be skeptical but fair when working on such stories.

In our conversations, I utilize the journalistic precepts examined throughout this book. Get the other side. Question the scientific information. Identify the group or individual making claims. Keep your personal view and your emotions out of the story. And so on. Generally my students have responded as one would expect. They are not as gullible or as naive as they were before, and their stories reflect their learning process. Most are becoming better electronic journalists.

But not all.

A few months ago, a student came to me with a story from another of those staged Washington news conferences. This time an environmental group was making pseudo-scientific and highly emotional accusations about pesticides in the water children were drinking.

As I reviewed the student's script, I asked: "Where is the other side?"

"What other side?" she replied somewhat belligerently. "How can anyone not be against poison in drinking water?"

I had to remind her of those traditional journalistic principles of fairness and objectivity, and warn her about emotional involvement, manipulation, and personal agendas.

I can only hope she will heed my advice and not allow emotions to overwhelm her in the future. However, despite our heightened awareness about the environmental beat, my students and I know we can still be exploited by the special-interest groups, politicians, and scientists promoting their own causes. That's because in covering environmental issues, the truth is not always clear.

As ABC's Barry Serafin says: "The curse of environmental reporting is the shades of gray. Often there are the same shades of truth in various viewpoints. Our ultimate job is to get as close to the truth as possible. That is neither black nor white but usually gray."

Notes

[1] Krier, James E., *Law and the Environment: Challenges for the Press* ["News Backgrounder" pamphlet] (Los Angeles: Foundation for American Communications, 1990).

[2] *Ibid.*

[3] Brookes, Warren T., "Study in political science," *Washington Times*, Dec. 5, 1990.

[4] Sullivan, James N., "Excellence and the environment," *Journal of Petroleum Technology*, Feb. 1990, p. 130.

[5] Potts, Mark, "Oil firms pour on 'earth first' message; image may profit from environmental efforts," *Washington Post*, Nov. 14, 1990.

[6] *Ibid.*

[7] Rosen, Joseph, quoted in Warren T. Brookes, "Sense and nonsense on the environment: Saving the earth is a fine thing but first you have to understand the issues," *Quill*, Jan./Feb. 1991. *See also* Timothy Egan, "Apple growers bruised and bitter after Alar scare," *New York Times*, July 9, 1991.

8 "How a PR firm executed the Alar scare" [Excerpts of memo by David Fenton], *Wall Street Journal*, Oct. 3, 1989.

9 Gifford, Bill, "Inside the environmental groups: Who they are. What they do. How well they do it. A consumer's guide to green giving," *Outside*, Sept. 1990.

10 Herstgaard, Mark, "Covering the world, ignoring the earth," *Rolling Stone*, Nov. 16, 1989.

11 Ryan, Teya, "Network earth: Advocacy, journalism, and the environment," *Gannett Center Journal*, Summer 1990, pp. 63, 69.

12 Meersman, Tom, "The advocacy debate: Does it miss the point?" *SEJournal*, Winter 1990-91, pp. 1, 5.

13 Detjen, Jim, "The traditionalist's tools (and a fistful of new ones)," *Gannett Center Journal*, Summer 1990, p. 76.

14 Reilly, William K., "Facing facts on the environment" [Commentary], *Washington Post*, Aug. 20, 1991.

15 Rowan, Ford, "Risk communication." In Ford Rowan, Erin Donovan, and Sarah Peasley, *Crisis Prevention, Management & Communications* (Washington: National Association of Manufacturers, 1991), p. 28.

16 Sapolsky, Harvey M., "The politics of risk," *Daedalus: Journal of the American Academy of Arts and Sciences*, Fall 1990, p. 91.

17 Rowan & Blewitt Inc. and Center for Risk Communication at Columbia University, *Risk Communication* [Workshop manual for plant managers] (Washington: Chemical Manufacturers Association, 1991), p. 16.

18 Reilly, William K., "Facing facts on the environment," *supra* note 14.

19 Cohn, Victor, "Reporters as gatekeepers." In Mike Moore, ed., *Health Risks and the Press* (Washington: The Media Institute, 1989), p. 38.

20 Cohn, Victor, *Reporting on Risk: Getting It Right in an Age of Risk* (Washington: The Media Institute, 1990), p. 7.

21 *Ibid.*, p. 8.

22 Sapolsky, Harvey M., "The politics of risk," *supra* note 16, pp. 90-91.

[23] Klaidman, Stephen, "How well the media report on health risks," *Daedalus: Journal of the American Academy of Arts and Sciences*, Fall 1990, p. 124.

[24] Friedman, Sharon, "Two decades of the environmental beat," *Gannett Center Journal*, Summer 1990, p. 17.

[25] Sibbison, Jim, "Dead fish and red herrings: How the EPA pollutes the news," *Columbia Journalism Review*, Nov./Dec. 1988, p. 26.

[26] Klaidman, Stephen, "How well the media report on health risks," *supra* note 23, p. 129.

[27] Friedman, Sharon, "Two decades of the environmental beat," *supra* note 24, p. 18.

[28] Hamilton, John Maxwell, "Survival alliances," *Gannett Center Journal*, Summer 1990, p. 11.

[29] Nelkin, Dorothy, "Journalism and science: The creative tension." In Mike Moore, ed., *Health Risks and the Press* (Washington: The Media Institute, 1989), p. 63.

[30] *Ibid.*

[31] Cohn, Victor, *Reporting on Risk*, *supra* note 20, p. 35.

[32] Cohn, Victor, "Reporters as gatekeepers," *supra* note 19, pp. 43-44.

[33] Sandman, Peter M., Michael Greenberg, and David B. Sachsman, *Risk Communication for Environmental News Sources*, quoted in Victor Cohn, *Reporting on Risk*, *supra* note 20, p. 18.

[34] Klaidman, Stephen, "How well the media report on health risks," *supra* note 23, pp. 124-125.

[35] Nelkin, Dorothy, "Journalism and science: The creative tension," *supra* note 29, p. 55.

[36] Weisskopf, Michael, "Rare pact reached to fight smog," *Washington Post*, Aug. 16, 1991.

Acknowledgments and Selected Bibliography

In the course of researching this monograph, I have talked with many people; read an abundance of printed material on the environment, environmental journalism, radio and television news, health, and science; and viewed dozens of network television news stories on environmental issues.

Some people have been quoted in this book, others have not. But all gave me an insight into the subject. I thank each of them for his or her help. I am particularly grateful to Roy Peter Clark, Roy Meyer, Doug Ramsey, Ford Rowan, Bud Ward, and Jim Willi who shared much of their organizations' environmental materials with me.

Personal sources and interviews

Doug Ballin, news director, WRAL-TV, Raleigh, N.C.

David Bartlett, president, Radio-Television News Directors Association, Washington.

Brad Bell, environmental reporter, WJLA-TV, Washington.

Anne Marie Bucholtz, environmental reporter, WMBD-TV, Peoria, Ill.

Kelly Burke, independent producer/reporter, Washington.

Eric Braun, executive vice president, Frank M. Magid Associates, Marion, Iowa.

Lisa Caputo, press secretary, Sen. Timothy Wirth (D-Colo.), Washington.

Roger Caras, special correspondent for animals and wildlife, ABC News, New York.

Roy Peter Clark, assistant director, The Poynter Institute, St. Petersburg, Fla.

Robert Currie, former producer, "Prime Time Live," ABC News, Washington.

George Dwyer, former producer, ABC News, Washington.

Sharon Friedman, chairperson, Department of Journalism, Lehigh University, Bethlehem, Pa.

George Glazier, vice president, Hill & Knowlton Inc., New York.

Wayne Godsey, general manager, KOAT-TV, Albuquerque, N.M.

Marty Haag, executive news director, WFAA-TV, Dallas.

Andrew Hershberger, reporter, WMUR-TV, Manchester, N.H.

Fred Jerome, director, Scientists Institute for Public Information, New York.

Robert Jordan, news director, KING-TV, Seattle.

Philip Kavits, senior director of radio and television, National Wildlife Federation, Washington.

S. Robert Lichter, co-director, Center for Media and Public Affairs, Washington.

William Line, assistant director of radio and television, National Wildlife Federation, Washington.

Robert Logan, director, Science Journalism Center, University of Missouri, Columbia, Mo.

Greg Lyons, investigative reporter, KRON-TV, San Francisco.

Allan Margolin, media director, Environmental Defense Fund, New York.

Amy McCombs, general manager, KRON-TV, San Francisco.

Roy Meyer, executive vice president, McHugh & Hoffman, Inc., McLean, Va.

Scott Miller, environmental reporter, KING-TV, Seattle.

Mackie Morris, consultant, Frank A. Magid Associates, Marion, Iowa.

Doug Ramsey, senior vice president, Foundation for American Communications, Los Angeles.

Dave Ropeik, environmental reporter, WCVB-TV, Boston.

Ford Rowan, attorney, Rowan & Blewitt Inc., Washington.

Barry Serafin, environmental correspondent, "World News Tonight," ABC News, Washington.

Philip Shabecoff, executive publisher and editor, *Greenwire*, Falls Church, Va.

James L. Snyder, vice president, Post-Newsweek Stations, Washington.

Kim Standish, publisher and editor, *The Rundown*, Ardmore, Pa.

Joyce Reid Sterling, news director, KDBC-TV, El Paso.

Rob Sunde, news director, ABC Radio, New York.

Eric Swanson, executive director, Radio and Television News Directors Foundation, Washington.

William Taylor, senior partner, Audience Research & Development, Dallas.

Rae Tyson, environmental reporter, *USA Today*, Arlington, Va.

Morris A. (Bud) Ward, executive director, Environmental Health Center, National Safety Council, Washington.

Kay Weeks, Peabody Awards, Grady School of Journalism, University of Georgia, Athens.

J. M. White, director, Science and Technology Center, University of Texas, Austin.

Ed Wickenheiser, news director, WGAL-TV, Lancaster, Pa.

James Willi, executive vice president, Audience Research & Development, Dallas.

William Winters, regional director of public affairs, General Motors Corp., New York.

Sen. Timothy Wirth (D-Colo.), Washington.

Charles Wolfe, news director, KIKK-Radio, Houston.

Gary Wordlaw, news director, WJLA-TV, Washington.

William Yeager, news director, KFWB-Radio, Los Angeles.

Books and monographs

Burger, Edward Jr., *Health Risks: The Challenge of Informing the Public* (Washington: The Media Institute, 1984).

Chemical Risks: Fears, Facts, and the Media (Washington: The Media Institute, 1985).

Chemicals, the Press, and the Public: A Journalist's Guide to Reporting on Chemicals in the Community (Washington: Environmental Health Center, National Safety Council, 1989).

Cohn, Victor, *Reporting on Risk: Getting It Right in an Age of Risk* (Washington: The Media Institute, 1990).

Corry, John, *TV News and the Dominant Culture* (Washington: The Media Institute, 1986).

Edelson, Edward, *The Journalist's Guide to Nuclear Energy* (Bethesda, Md.: Atomic Industrial Forum, 1985).

Moore, Mike, ed., *Health Risks and the Press: Perspectives on Media Coverage of Risk Assessment and Health* (Washington: The Media Institute, 1989).

Nuclear Phobia—Phobic Thinking About Nuclear Power: A Discussion with Robert L. DuPont, M.D. (Washington: The Media Institute, 1980).

Television Evening News Covers Nuclear Energy: A Ten-Year Perspective (Washington: The Media Institute, 1979).

Webster's New Collegiate Dictionary (Springfield, Mass.: G. & C. Merriam Co., 1979).

When Disaster Strikes: A Handbook for the Media (Washington: Federal Emergency Management Agency, Sept. 1985).

Journal and magazine articles

Bertram, Amy, "Environment beat challenges media," *Electronic Media*, Dec. 17, 1990.

Brookes, Warren T., "Sense and nonsense on the environment: Saving the earth is a fine thing but first you have to understand the issues," *Quill*, Jan./Feb. 1991.

Browning, Graeme, "Taking some risks: Washington's fiscal constraints are driving a renewed search for ways to get more risk reduction for the regulatory buck; but skeptics label risk assessment a 'sham science,'" *National Journal*, June 1, 1991.

Chadwick, Kyle, "Big suits: Ouvil et al v. CBS et al," *American Lawyer*, Jan./Feb. 1991.

"Covering the environment" [Special issue], *Gannett Center Journal*, Summer 1990.

Denne, Lorianne, "Apple commission won't join '60 Minutes' suit," *Puget Sound Business Journal*, Jan. 21, 1991.

Fairlie, Henry, "Fear of living: America's morbid aversion to risk," *New Republic*, Jan. 23, 1989.

Fitzgerald, Mike and Brent Shearer, "Judgment call: How far down the tobacco road?" *Columbia Journalism Review*, July/Aug. 1991.

Friedrich, Otto, "Scrubbing the skies: After 13 years of frustration, the Senate finally strikes a deal to clean the air—but business and environmentalists are still fighting," *Time*, April 16, 1990.

Gifford, Bill, "Inside the environmental groups: Who they are. What they do. How well they do it. A consumer's guide to green giving," *Outside*, Sept. 1990.

Hertsgaard, Mark, "Covering the world, ignoring the earth," *Rolling Stone*, Nov. 16, 1989.

Hertsgaard, Mark, "The 60 minute man: How Don Hewitt keeps his ratings up," *Rolling Stone*, May 30, 1991.

Kleiner, Art, "Brundtland's legacy: Can corporations really practice environmentalism while fattening their profit margins?" *Garbage*, Sept./Oct. 1990.

Marianyi, Esther, "Marching to a new beat: Environmental reporters hit the pulse of public concern and grab the spotlight," *Byline: Northwestern's Journalism Review*, Spring 1990.

McDermott, Jeanne, "Some heartland farmers just say no to chemicals," *Smithsonian*, April 1990.

Mermigas, Diane, "King media sale to aid environment," *Electronic Media*, Aug. 27, 1990.

"Money from pollution suits can follow a winding course," *Insight*, Feb. 18, 1991.

Moore, Mike, "The quest for certainty," *Quill*, Jan./Feb. 1991.

Nelson, Robert H., "Tom Hayden, meet Adam Smith and Thomas Aquinas: Why can't business people resist environmentalists' extreme demands? They fail to understand they are dealing with a religion, not with politics or economics," *Forbes*, Oct. 29, 1990.

"Newsrooms hit paydirt with environment," *Broadcasting*, June 3, 1991.

"The 1990 directory to environmental organizations," *Buzzworm: The Environmental Journal*, May/June 1990.

Norris, Eileen, "Kurtis using media to help clean up," *Electronic Media*, Dec. 17, 1990.

"Risk" [Special issue], *Daedalus: Journal of the American Academy of Arts and Sciences*, Fall 1990.

Robotham, Rosemarie, "Not in my backyard," *Omni Magazine*, Sept. 1989.

Sabreen, Richard, "How Three Mile Island started the news feed business," *Communicator*, May 1991.

Sibbison, Jim, "Dead fish and red herrings: How the EPA pollutes the news," *Columbia Journalism Review*, Nov./Dec. 1988.

Spencer, Cathy, "Help wanted: An activist's guide to a better earth," *Omni Magazine*, Sept. 1989.

Stocking, Holly and Jennifer Pease Leonard, "The greening of the press," *Columbia Journalism Review*, Nov./Dec. 1990.

Sullivan, James N., "Excellence and the environment," *Journal of Petroleum Technology*, Feb. 1990.

Titone, Julie, "Shop talk at thirty: Ten commandments for environmental reporters," *Editor and Publisher*, Sept. 22, 1990.

Tyson, Rae, "Reporting can be hazardous to your health," *Washington Journalism Review*, Nov. 1989.

Ward, Morris A., "Communicating on environmental risk," *The Environmental Forum*, Jan. 1986.

Williams, Bob, "Neodruid counteroffensive," *Oil & Gas Journal*, Dec. 10, 1990.

Newsletters

Environment Writer [monthly publication of the Environmental Health Center, National Safety Council, Washington]. *See* Oct. 1990; Nov. 1990; Dec. 1990; Feb. 1991; Mar. 1991; April 1991; May 1991.

Friedman, Sharon and James Detjen, "CFJ tip sheet: Covering environmental news," *CFJ Newsletter* [quarterly publication of the Center for Foreign Journalists, Reston, Va.], Winter 1990.

"Preserving the planet: Media coverage of the environment during 1989," *Media Monitor* [publication of the Center for Media and Public Affairs, Washington], April 1990.

The Rundown [weekly publication of Standish Publishing Co., Ardmore, Pa.]. *See* July 28, 1986; Aug. 11, 1986; Dec. 15, 1986; Jan. 18, 1988; June 20, 1988; July 11, 1988; Sept. 26, 1988; May 22, 1989; June 5, 1989; Sept. 11, 1989; Nov. 20, 1989; Mar. 12, 1990; May 7, 1990. *See also* May 1, 1989; July 3, 1989; Oct. 2, 1989; Nov. 27, 1989; Feb. 6, 1990; Mar. 6, 1990; April 16, 1990; Aug. 20, 1990; April 15, 1991, Mar. 11, 1991.

SEJournal [quarterly publication of the Society of Environmental Journalists, Washington]. *See* Fall 1990; Winter 1990/91; Spring/Summer 1991.

Newspaper articles

"Alar scare: Case study in media's skewed reality," *Wall Street Journal*, April 20, 1989.

Anthan, George, "EPA caught in crossfire over pesticide use," Gannett News Service, Feb. 24, 1991.

Associated Press, "After scare, suit by apple farmers," *New York Times*, Nov. 29, 1990.

Associated Press, "Apple growers sue over CBS Alar report," *Chicago Tribune*, Nov. 29, 1990.

Balz, Dan, "Politicians trying to adapt" [Part three of series "Going Green"], *Washington Post*, April 20, 1990.

Barber, Lionel, "The un-greening of America," *Financial Times*, April 13, 1991.

Berry, John M., "The owl's golden egg: Environmentalism could boost lumber profits and prices," *Washington Post*, Aug. 4, 1991.

Booth, William, "Study: Logging cut needed to save Northwest forests, move could cost 38,000 jobs, panel says," *Washington Post*, July 25, 1991.

Booth, William and D'Vera Cohn, "Sharing the environmental burden: Many Americans confused about how to put concern into action" [Part one of series "Going Green"], *Washington Post*, April 18, 1990.

Bowie, Liz, "Scientists debate how to evaluate chemicals' risk," *Baltimore Sun*, Sept. 1, 1991.

Brookes, Warren T., "Big green's lethal secret: Why cancer risk would rise," *Washington Times*, Oct. 15, 1990.

Brookes, Warren T., "EPA overlooking the greater risk?" *Washington Times*, May 13, 1991.

Brookes, Warren T., "Great green scam?" *Washington Times*, Jan. 28, 1991.

Brookes, Warren T., "Study in political science" [Part one of three-part commentary series], *Washington Times*, Dec. 5, 1990.

Brooks, David, "Journalists and others for saving the planet," *Wall Street Journal*, Oct. 5, 1989.

Cannon, Lou, "Saw-toothed despair leaves mark on northwestern loggers," *Washington Post*, July 27, 1991.

"CBS takes the acid test" [Editorial], *Washington Times*, Jan. 7, 1991.

Chase, Marilyn, "A new cancer drug may extend lives—at cost of rare trees; that angers conservationists who say Taxol extraction endangers the prized yew," *Wall Street Journal*, April 19, 1991.

Dannemeyer, William E. (R-Calif.), "Commentary: Challenging the Clean Air Act on basis of costs and benefits: An opponent argues that the act will reduce economic growth, impede competitiveness, and force some employers to relocate offshore," *Los Angeles Times*, Nov. 25, 1990.

Dietrich, Bill, "Dixy Lee Ray re-opens fire on eco-activists," *Seattle Times*, March 4, 1991.

Dolan, Maura (*Los Angeles Times*), "New studies cast doubts on environmentalist credos," *Indianapolis Star*, March 24, 1991.

Egan, Timothy, "Apple growers bruised and bitter after Alar scare," *New York Times*, July 9, 1991.

Gladwell, Malcolm, "Some fear bad precedent in Alar alarm; scientists criticize pulling of apples without proof of danger," *Washington Post*, April 19, 1989.

Gutfeld, Rose, "Eight of 10 Americans are environmentalists, at least so they say," *Wall Street Journal*, Aug. 2, 1991.

Harwood, Richard, "Ombudsman: Media mystery tour," *Washington Post*, March 3, 1991.

"How a PR firm executed the Alar scare" [Excerpts of memo by David Fenton], *Wall Street Journal*, Oct. 3, 1989.

Kuhn, Thomas R., "Clean-air politics" [Letter to the editor], *Christian Science Monitor*, April 6, 1990.

Kurtz, Howard, "Is acid rain a tempest in news media teapot? Study questioning harm gets little attention," *Washington Post*, Jan. 14, 1991.

Lancaster, John, "The environmentalist as insider: National Wildlife Federation President Jay Hair thinks working within the system is the only way to go," *Washington Post Magazine*, Aug. 4, 1991.

Lancaster, John, "Environmentalists hail freeze on timber sales to guard owl; industry group warns of escalating lumber prices," *Washington Post*, May 25, 1991.

Lancaster, John, "Grass-roots activists confront pollution on home front," *Washington Post*, April 19, 1990.

ACKNOWLEDGMENTS AND SELECTED BIBLIOGRAPHY 93

Lancaster, John, "War and recession taking toll on national environmental organizations," *Washington Post*, Feb. 15, 1991.

Lancaster, John, "Western industries fuel grass-roots drive for 'wise use' of resources," *Washington Post*, May 16, 1991.

Lancaster, John, "Would 'green' taxes change a society's polluting ways?" *Washington Post*, Feb. 12, 1991.

"Law: Love Canal court papers to be opened," *Wall Street Journal*, May 15, 1991.

Nogaki, Sylvia Weiland, "Labor: Apple farm pesticides persist—demonstrators invoke Alar to push growers into talks," *Seattle Times*, March 20, 1991.

Okie, Susan, "Panel seeks tougher medical research rules; House report cites alleged misconduct including scientists' financial conflict of interest," *Washington Post*, Sept. 9, 1990.

Perlman, Adam, "U.S. urged to lead world conservation effort," *Boston Globe*, Sept. 17, 1989.

Pollack, Andrew, "Moving fast to protect ozone layer," *New York Times*, May 15, 1991.

"Pollution's progress" [Editorial], *Wall Street Journal*, June 6, 1991.

Potts, Mark, "Oil firms pour on 'earth first' message; image may profit from environmental efforts," *Washington Post*, Nov. 14, 1990.

Puzo, Daniel P., "Food bites back: Issues of 1990," *Los Angeles Times*, Jan. 3, 1991.

Reilly, William K., "Facing facts on the environment" [Commentary], *Washington Post*, Aug. 20, 1991.

"Revenge of the killer apples" [Editorial], *Washington Times*, March 27, 1991.

Robbins, Jim, "Are cowboys killing the West?" *USA Weekend*, April 19-21, 1991.

Schmid, Randolph, "Climate warning," Associated Press, Sept. 16, 1989.

Schneider, Keith, "U.S. officials say dangers of dioxin were exaggerated," *New York Times*, Aug. 15, 1991.

Shabecoff, Philip, "Acid rain report unleashes a torrent of criticism," *New York Times*, March 20, 1990.

Shabecoff, Philip, "Apple chemical being removed in U.S. market," *New York Times*, June 3, 1989.

Shabecoff, Philip, "Apple scare of '89 didn't kill market," *New York Times*, Nov. 13, 1990.

Shabecoff, Philip, "3 U.S. agencies, to allay public's fears, declare apples safe," *New York Times*, May 17, 1989.

Silk, Leonard (New York Times News Service), "U.S. science community suffers crisis of confidence," *Indianapolis Star*, March 24, 1991.

Stammer, Larry (*Los Angeles Times*), "Lack of action on environmental problems alarms scientists," *Louisville Courier-Journal*, Sept. 17, 1989.

Stevens, William K., "Ozone loss over U.S. is found to be twice as bad as predicted; EPA chief says rate is stunning and disturbing," *New York Times*, April 5, 1991.

ACKNOWLEDGMENTS AND SELECTED BIBLIOGRAPHY 95

Stevens, William K., "What really threatens the environment? Official seeks to start a debate over the nation's goals," *New York Times*, Jan. 29, 1991.

Stipp, David, "Super waste? Throwing good money at bad water yields scant improvement," *Wall Street Journal*, May 15, 1991.

Sugarman, Carole, "The alarm over Alar; What's a consumer to do about apples?" *Washington Post*, March 8, 1989.

"Warming up to the facts" [Editorial], *Wall Street Journal*, Jan. 11, 1991.

Weingarten, Paul, "Apple growers to stop using Alar," *Chicago Tribune*, May 16, 1989.

Weisskopf, Michael, "Advocacy groups leading the way" [Part two of series "Going Green"], *Washington Post*, April 19, 1990.

Weisskopf, Michael, "Rare pact reached to fight smog," *Washington Post*, Aug. 16, 1991.

Weisskopf, Michael, "Rewriting the book on wetlands: Scientists wash hands of White House's definition of protected areas," *Washington Post*, May 3, 1991.

Weisskopf, Michael, "Wetlands protection and the struggle over environmental policy," *Washington Post*, Aug. 8, 1991.

Weisskopf, Michael, "With pen, Bush to seal administration split on Clean Air Act," *Washington Post*, Nov. 15, 1990.

Williams, Walter E. (Creators Syndicate), "Environmental threat," *Indianapolis News*, June 8, 1991.

Wright, Karen (*Science* magazine), "Heating the global warming debate," *New York Times*, Feb. 3, 1991.

Papers, manuals, and miscellaneous

Bardack, Mark and Janet Koewler, "Health risks and the media," unpublished graduate seminar paper, Northwestern University, Medill School of Journalism Washington Program, 1990.

D'Innocenzio, Anne and Lisa Eldridge, "The Alar crisis: How the media handled the bad apples," unpublished graduate seminar paper, Northwestern University, Medill School of Journalism Washington Program, 1989.

Environmental Reporting Seminar for Broadcast and Print Reporters [Seminar manual] (St. Petersburg, Fla.: The Poynter Institute for Media Studies, 1991).

The E-Team [Client manual] (Dallas: Audience Research & Development, 1989).

Examples of Franchises for the '90s ["Issues of the '90s" pamphlet] (McLean, Va.: McHugh & Hoffman, Inc., 1990).

Finkel, Adam M., "Are we ready for 'worst-first' environmental protection?" [Commentary] (Washington: Resources for the Future, 1991).

Friedman, Sharon M. and Carol L. Rogers, eds., *Environmental Risk Reporting: The Science and the Coverage* [Workshop proceedings] (Bethlehem, Pa.: Lehigh University, 1991).

In Celebration of Coal [Transcription of Western Fuels Association 16th annual energy conference, Garden City, Kan., July 25-26, 1990] (Washington: Western Fuels Association, 1990).

Janezich, Lawrence, "The press and the First Amendment" [Speech by superintendent of U.S. Senate radio-television gallery to Orange County (Calif.) Bar Association], May 1, 1991.

Krier, James E., *Law and the Environment: Challenges for the Press* ["News Backgrounder" pamphlet] (Los Angeles: Foundation for American Communications, 1990).

Matusik, Kathleen and Margaret Ann Miller, "Crisis communication: How the press covers the EPA and its toxic release inventory," unpublished graduate seminar paper, Northwestern University, Medill School of Journalism Washington Program, 1989.

Quintanilla, Ray and Sara Parker, "The press' responses to a crisis situation. The Alar controversy: Was it overblown?" unpublished graduate seminar paper, Northwestern University, Medill School of Journalism Washington Program, 1990.

Rowan & Blewitt Inc. and Center for Risk Communication at Columbia University, *Risk Communication* [Workshop manual for plant managers] (Washington: Chemical Manufacturers Association, 1991).

Wirth, Timothy E. (D-Colo.), "The environmental imperative" [Commencement address at Harvard College], June 5, 1991.

Index

ABC, 8, 17, 24, 25, 26, 27, 42, 67, 72, 75
Alar, 5, 21, 22, 56, 66
Alaska, 38, 43
   Prince William Sound, 38
Alexander, Charles, 27
Amazon, 50
"American Agenda," 42
American Forest Resources Alliance, 11
Associated Press, 22, 72
Athens, Art, 45, 46, 47
Atlanta, Ga., 41
Audience Research & Development, 48, 49
Ballin, Doug, 43, 49
Baltimore, Md., 37, 44
Bartlett, David, viii, 46
Baskin, Roberta, 45
Baton Rouge, La., 44
Bell, Brad, 44, 45, 52
Bhopal, India, 37
Boston, 18, 28, 42, 43, 44, 68, 69, 73

Bradley, Ed, 21
Braun, Eric, 49, 50
Brazil, 51, 73
Brookes, Warren, 4, 16, 24, 25
Bucholtz, Anne Marie, 44
Buffalo, N.Y., 39
Burke, Kelly, 35
Bush, President George, 25, 60
Bush Administration, 12, 13, 63
Cable News Network, 32, 37, 42, 72
   see "Network Earth"
California, 49
Canada, 43
Caras, Roger, 8, 24, 27, 42, 67
Carter Administration, 57
CBS, 17, 22, 26, 36, 41, 72, 73
Center for Media and Public Affairs, 17, 21, 28, 63
Chemicals, the Press, and the Public, 4, 10
Chernobyl, 35, 38
Chevron Corporation, 17
Clean Air Act, 9, 10, 12, 13, 18, 74

Cohn, Victor, 4, 60, 65, 67
Columbia-DuPont, 41
Columbia Journalism Review, 4, 63
Columbia University, 58
   Center for Risk Communication, 58
Conservation Foundation/World
   Wildlife Fund, 19
Cornell University, 64, 66
Covello, Vincent, 58
Creators Syndicate, 24
Cronkite, Walter, 36
Dallas, Tex., 49
Dayton, Ohio, 38
Deer Park, Tex., 47
Department of Agriculture, 12, 21
   see U.S. Forest Service
Department of the Interior, 12
   Bureau of Land Management, 12
   Bureau of Mines, 12
   see National Park Service
Denver, 45
Detjen, Jim, 4, 28, 29
Detroit News, 24
"Doctor Earth," 51
Ducks Unlimited, 19, 20
DuPont, Robert, 35
"E-Team," 48, 51
Earth Day, 9, 48, 49
Earth First, 20
Earth Summit, 73
Egan, Timothy, 77
El Paso, Tex., 41
England, 32
Environmental Defense Fund, 25
Environmental Health Center, 4, 10, 46
Environmental Protection Agency, 9, 15, 16, 21, 22, 39, 40, 53, 54, 57, 58, 59, 60, 63, 64, 71
   Science Advisory Board, 16, 59
Environmental Reporting Forum, vii, viii, 71
Environment Writer, 4, 10, 70
Eureka Springs, Ark., 40
Falls Church, Va., 71

Fenton, David, 22
Fenton Communications, 22
Food and Drug Administration, 21
Foundation for American
   Communications, 71
Forbes, 25
Francis, Michael, 18
Friedman, Sharon, 36, 63, 64, 67, 69
Gannett Center for Media Studies, 4
Gannett Center Journal, 4, 27, 28
Gannett Company, 44
Gannett News Service, 37
General Motors Corporation, 68
Georgetown University, 62
   Kennedy Institute of Ethics, 62
Germany, 73
Gifford, Bill, 23
"Green Team, The," 51
Greenpeace, 20
Greenwire, 13, 71
Haag, Marty, 50
Hamilton, John Maxwell, 64
Harris, Byron, 50
Harrisburg, Pa., 5, 35
"Harvest of Shame," 27
Hathaway, Janet, 22
Hattoway, Bob, 18
Hayes, Erin, 40, 41, 42
Health Risks and the Press, 4
Hershey Medical Center, 37
Hertsgaard, Mark, 24, 25, 28
Hill and Knowlton Inc., 56
Hiroshima, 36
Hodgkin's Disease, 37
Hollenhorst, John, 49
Hooker Chemical Company, 39
Houston, Tex., 44, 46, 47
Inquiry, 71
Izaak Walton League, 19
Japan, 32
Kansas City, 48
Kavits, Phil, 19, 20, 22, 25
KCNC-TV, 45
KDBC-TV, 41

Kemeny Commission, 36, *see*
  President's Commission on the
  Accident at Three Mile Island
KFWB-Radio, 46
KGO-TV, 44
  "The Naturalists," 44, 51
KIKK-Radio, 46
KING-TV, 43, 44, 73
Klaidman, Stephen, 62, 63, 64, 66, 67
Krier, James E., 15
KRON-TV, 42
  "Target 4," 42
KSL-TV, 49
KTRK-TV, 44
Kuwait, 38
KYTV, 40
Lake Erie, 5
Lancaster, Pa., 36
Lehigh University, 36, 63, 69
Leslie, Bill, 43
Lichter, S. Robert, 28
Linden, Dr. Tom, 42
Long Island, 33
Los Angeles, 46, 71
Los Angeles Times, 72
Love Canal, 39, 40
Lyon, Greg, 42
Magid Associates, Frank N., 48, 49
Maine, 49
Maines, Patrick D., viii
Margolin, Allan, 25
Massachusetts Institute of Technology, 58, 61
Mauro, Tony, 37
McCombs, Amy, 43
McH⎵gh & Hoffman, Inc., 48, 49
⎵ ⎵ ⎵4
⎵ ⎵ ⎵nformation Project, 47
Media Institute, The, vii, viii, 4, 71
Medill News Service, 5
Meersman, Tom, 28, 46
Meyer, Roy, 49, 50
Miami Herald, 72
Michigan, 5
Middletown, Pa., 36

Miller, Dr. Kenneth, 37
Miller, Scott, 43, 44, 73
Minnesota Public Radio, 28, 46
Mitchell, Andrea, 26
Moore, Mike, 4
Morris, Mackie, 49
Moynihan (D-N.Y.), Daniel Patrick, 59
Murrow, Edward R., 27
Nader, Ralph, 36
National Academy of Sciences, 21
  Issues in Science and Technology, 21
National Acid Precipitation
  Assessment Program, 13, 16
National Audubon Society, 19
National Institutes of Health, 65
National Park Service, 11, 12
National Public Radio, 46
National Safety Council, 4, 10
  see Environmental Health Center
National Wildlife Federation, 19, 20, 21, 22, 25
Natural Resources Defense Council, 19, 21, 22
  "Intolerable risk: Pesticides in our children's food," 21
  "Mothers and Others for Pesticide Limits," 21
Nature Conservancy, 19
NBC, 17, 26, 57, 72
Nelkin, Dorothy, 64, 66, 67
Nelson, Gaylord, 9
"Network Earth," 27
New England, 43
New York, 14, 21, 37, 45, 68, 71, 72
  see Buffalo, Long Island, Love Canal, Niagara Falls
New York Times, 4, 13, 22, 35, 72, 72-73, 73, 77
Newsweek, 17, 72
Nexis, 4
Niagara Falls, N.Y., 39
Niagara Gazette, 40
Nickles (R-Okla.), Senator Don, 13
Nielson, John, 46

North Carolina, 43
Northwestern University, 5, 74
Oklahoma City, 13
Olympic National Park, 11
Orange County, Calif., 33
Oregon, 11, 49
Outside Magazine, 20, 23
Ozarks, 40
PCB, 4
Peabody Awards, 45
Pearson, Ian, 42
Peoria, Ill., 44
Persian Gulf War, 32, 49
Philadelphia, 37
Philadelphia Inquirer, 4, 28
Pittsburgh, 37
Post-Newsweek Stations, 50
Potter, Ned, 42
Poynter Institute, 71
President's Commission on the Accident at Three Mile Island, 36
 Task Force on the Public's Right to Information, 36
Public Broadcasting Service, 26
Pyle, Barbara, 26
Quill, 4, 12
Quimbach, Charles, 46
Radio-Television News Directors Association, 13, 38, 43, 46, 48
 Communicator, 46
Radio and Television News Directors Foundation, vii, viii, 19, 31-32, 71
Raleigh, N.C., 42, 49
Reagan/Bush Administration, 64
Reid, Joyce *see* Joyce Reid Sterling
Reilly, William K., 54, 59
"Reporter's Guide to the Clean Air Act," 10
Reporting on Risk, 4
Risk Communication for Environmental News Sources, 65
Rio de Janiero, 73
Rolling Stone, 24, 25
Ropeik, Dave, 18, 28, 43, 44, 68, 69, 70, 73

Roper poll, 59
Rosen, Dr. Joseph, 21
Rowan, Ford, 57, 62, 65
Rundown, The, 42, 48
Russia, 38
 see Chernobyl
Rutgers University, 21, 65
Ryan, Teya, 27
St. Paul, Minn., 46
St. Petersburg, Fla., 71
Salt Lake City, Utah, 49
San Francisco, 42, 44
Sapolsky, Harvey M., 58, 61
Schultz, Ernie, 13, 14
Scientists Institute for Public Information, 71
Scripps-Howard, 45
Sea Shepherd Conservation Society, 20
Seattle, Wash., 43, 73
Serafin, Barry, 42, 75
Shabecoff, Philip, 4, 13
Sibbison, Jim, 63, 64
Sierra Club, 18, 19
"60 Minutes," 12, 21, 22
Smithsonian Institution, 26, 72
Snyder, James L., 50
Society of Environmental Journalists, 4, 10, 27, 28, 46, 71
 SEJournal, 28, 71
Society of Professional Journalists, 43
Springfield, Mo., 40, 41
Stahl, Leslie, 72, 73
Standish, Kim, 42, 48
Sterling, Joyce Reid, 40, 41, 42
Streep, Meryl, 21
Sullivan, James N., 17
Superfund, 57
Swanson, Eric, 19, 20
Three Mile Island, 5, 34, 35, 36, 37, 40, 56
Time Magazine, 17, 27
Time-Warner Corporation, 25
Turner, Ted, 26, 42
Turner Broadcasting Inc., 25, 26, 27
Turner Broadcasting System, 26

Twentieth Century Fund, 60
Tyson, Rae, 4, 40, 68
United Nations, 73
United States, 16, 18, 32, 39, 41, 46, 59
U.S. government, 17
USA Today, 4, 37, 40, 68, 72
U.S. Congress, 9, 11, 13, 26, 58, 59, 63, 71
U.S. Forest Service, 12
U.S. House of Representatives, 13
House Government Operations Committee, 65
U.S. News and World Report, 17
U.S. Senate, 13, 59
University of Michigan, 15, 71
Meeman Archive, 71
University of Missouri, 71
Science Journalism Center, 71
Valdez, 38
Vietnam, 34
Wall Street Journal, 22, 72
Ward, Morris A. (Bud), 4, 10, 16, 25, 46, 47, 57, 58, 70, 71
Washington State, 11, 22, 49
Washington, D.C., viii, 4, 5, 14, 15, 17, 21, 22, 23, 25, 26, 35, 37, 44, 46, 64, 72, 73, 75
Washington Post, 12, 18, 59, 60, 72, 73, 74
Washington Times, 24
WBRZ-TV, 44
WBZ-TV, 44
WCBS-Radio, 45, 46

WCVB-TV, 18, 28, 42, 43, 44, 68, 69
Webster's New Collegiate Dictionary, 7
Weisskopf, Michael, 74
WFAA-TV, 49
WGAL-TV, 36
WHIO-TV, 38
White House, 9, 72
Wickenheiser, Ed, 35, 36
Wilderness Society, 18, 19
Willi, Jim, 49
Winters, Bill, 68
Wisconsin, 9
Wisconsin Public Radio, 46
WJLA-TV, 44, 45, 52
WLVI-TV, 44
"Greenwatch," 44
WMAR-TV, 44
WMBD-TV, 44
"Earth Watch," 44
Wolfe, Chuck, 46, 47
World Bank, 64
"World News Tonight," 42
Wordlaw, Gary, 45, 52
WRAL-TV, 42, 43, 49
"Save our Sounds," 43
"Troubled Waters," 43
WRC-TV, 35
WSBA, 35
Wyoming, 38
Yankelovich poll, 17
Yeager, Bill, 46
Yellowstone National Park, 38, 45
York, Pa., 35

Lou Prato is a veteran journalist, radio and television news director, and educator. Since 1983 he has been director of Washington Graduate Broadcast Programs for Northwestern University's Medill School of Journalism. An associate professor of journalism, he also serves as director of the Medill News Service in Washington.

From 1977 to 1983 Mr. Prato was news director of WDTN-TV in Dayton, Ohio. In the mid-1970s he was Midwest bureau chief of NBC-Radio News in Chicago. He began his broadcast career in Pittsburgh and in 1972 took his first news director's position at the NBC-TV affiliate in Detroit.

A former reporter for the Associated Press, Mr. Prato writes frequently for media trade publications and is a regular columnist for *Washington Journalism Review*. He has served on the board of directors of the Radio-Television News Directors Association since 1977.

Covering the Environmental Beat was produced by David P. Taggart. Sharon Anthony provided editorial assistance and compiled the index.

A publication of the Environmental Reporting Forum
Richard T. Kaplar, General Editor

The Radio and Television News Directors Foundation (RTNDF) is a nonprofit charitable foundation that conducts programs aimed at improving the practice of radio and television journalism. The RTNDF cooperates on certain educational programs with the Radio-Television News Directors Association, a nonprofit professional organization of 3,600 broadcast news executives, producers, writers, reporters, students, and educators. For more information contact David Bartlett, President, Radio and Television News Directors Foundation, 1000 Connecticut Ave., N.W., Washington, D.C. 20036.

The Media Institute is a nonprofit, tax-exempt research foundation that seeks to foster freedom of speech, a competitive communications industry, and excellence in journalism. The Institute publishes studies, conducts conferences, and sponsors programs on a host of communications policy issues. The Institute is supported by a wide range of foundations, corporations, associations, and individuals. To support the work of the Institute, or for further information, contact Patrick D. Maines, President, The Media Institute, 1000 Potomac Street, N.W., Washington, D.C. 20007.